Good Kids

Good Kids

How You and Your Kids Can
Successfully Navigate the Teen Years

• •

Nick Stinnett

Michael O'Donnell

DOUBLEDAY

NEW YORK • LONDON • TORONTO • SYDNEY • AUCKLAND

PUBLISHED BY DOUBLEDAY

a division of Bantam Doubleday Dell Publishing Group, Inc.

1540 Broadway, New York, New York 10036

DOUBLEDAY and the portrayal of an anchor with a dolphin are trademarks of
Doubleday, a division of Bantam Doubleday Dell Publishing Group, Inc.

Book design by Jessica Shatan

Library of Congress Cataloging-in-Publication Data

Stinnett, Nick.
    Good kids : how you and your kids can successfully navigate the teen years / Nick
Stinnett, Michael O'Donnell. — 1st ed.
        p.   cm.
    Includes index.
    1. Teenagers—United States—Case studies. 2. Success in adolescence—United States—
Case studies. 3. Parent and teenager—United States. I. O'Donnell, Michael (Michael Alan),
1956–   . II. Title.
HQ796.S84   1996
649'.125—dc20   96-15986
                                                                                            CIP

ISBN 0-385-48443-7

Printed in the United States of America
November 1996
First Edition
10   9   8   7   6   5   4   3   2   1

It is with love that we dedicate this book to the children of our two families—David Stinnett and Joseph Stinnett; Patrick O'Donnell and Kayla O'Donnell.

And we would like to express our gratitude to the many adolescents across the nation who shared with us the secrets of their well-being. Their wisdom has given us insight concerning what is important to the well-being of individuals at any age as well as to the health and survival of a society.

Acknowledgments

We wish to acknowledge first of all the support and encouragement of our families. Without these special relationships this book would never have evolved.

We are both fortunate to find ourselves in university environments where growth is a goal and encouragement an abundant resource. Sincere appreciation is expressed to Becky Ladewig and Tommie Hamner of the Department of Human Development and Family Studies at the University of Alabama; and to Judy Bonner, Dean of the College of Human Environmental Sciences at the University of Alabama.

Appreciation is also expressed to Marianna Rasco, Chair of the Department of Family and Consumer Sciences at Abilene Christian University. Colleagues and friends make the way meaningful and enjoyable. It is a pleasure to work with such a fine group of people: Mary Liz Curtner-Smith, Sally Edwards, Ann Fulmer, Carmen Hudson, Terri Huizinga, Peggy Jessee, Eileen MaloneBeach, Dee Morgan, and Stephen Thoma.

Good research costs money and requires support, cooperation, and time from others. We have been generously supported by the National Family Life Institute; the Texas 4-H and Youth Development and Family Life Programs and the Texas Agricultural Extension Service; and the Center for Excellence at Tennessee State University. A sincere thank you to Barbara Nye, Director of the Center for Excellence.

We particularly wish to thank Greg Johnson for all of his contributions. Finally, we express our deep appreciation to Mark Fretz, Senior Editor, and Christian Heller-Schoenberg, Associate Editor, Doubleday, and to the entire editorial staff of Doubleday for their helpful assistance and encouragement.

Contents

Introduction

One teen at a time, please, is the hope held out by every parent in America. After all, it's hard enough raising one thirteen-year-old, but two? Forget it!

My (Michael O'Donnell) parents had no choice, however. God had blessed them (or burdened them, depending upon your point of view) with identical twin boys, me and my brother, Richard. We were nicknamed "double trouble," a well-earned title that stuck with us throughout high school.

When we were young, Richard and I were so alike that even my father could not tell us apart. To discipline us, my father would shout our names until we both assembled at his feet. Then, pointing to one of us, he would ask, "Now, which one are you? Michael or Richard?" Soon after the discovery of the correct twin to be punished, a penalty for wrongdoing would begin.

Well, it didn't take me long to figure out that, since my father couldn't tell us apart, aiding him in his apparent disability only quickened the inevitable spanking and lecture that followed. A new strategy was necessary. At this point, I need to tell you that my mother would help my father by writing the name of the twin to be disciplined on a note pad next to the kitchen phone. When my father would come home late from work, he'd simply read the name of the disobedient twin, climb the stairs to the second floor, and pull me (who always slept on the top bunk) or my brother (who slept on the bottom) from our deep sleep to administer justice. This, by the way, added a whole new dimension to the words, "Wait till your father gets home!"

To continue the story: One day when I was eight years old, I broke a living-room lamp. I had been told to stay a safe distance from the lamp to avoid just such an accident, but I had disobeyed. I was in need of reproach. So my mother wrote my name on the infamous pad of paper. After dinner and a bath, Richard and I were sent upstairs to bed. Awake on the top bunk, I awaited my doom. And then it struck me! *If only I could get Richard to sleep on the top bunk.*

Because we were avid fans of the hit TV show "The Adventures of Superman," I decided to arouse my brother's curiosity by pretending to be "the Man of Steel." With the top bunk creating the illusion of flying over the great Metropolis, I said in low tones (but loud enough for my brother to hear), "Faster than a speeding bullet, more powerful than a locomotive, able to leap tall buildings with a single bound . . . it's SUPERMAN!"

"Hey, what are you doing?" he asked.

"Nothing, just go to sleep," I replied.

"No, tell me. Tell me."

Baiting him, I continued: "I'm pretending to be Superman, flying over the city. See, by swinging my arms out over the bed, I feel like I'm really in the air. . . . Da dum . . . da da da dum . . . Faster than a speeding bullet . . . whee!"

As predicted, Richard began to plead, "Let me play, please."

"No, only me."

"Come on! Just for a little while, *please*?!"

"Oh, all right." I gave in to his request with the one condition that he stay on the top bed for the entire night—something he previously would never do. But tonight he decided to make an exception, and a costly one at that. Why, I could barely contain my laughter as Richard began the Superman antics where I left off.

"More powerful than a locomotive . . . Da dum . . . da da da da dum."

It was about ten o'clock when our father came home. I can still remember his footsteps pounding up the stairs and heading for our room. The anticipation had kept me awake while my unsuspecting twin had long since fallen asleep. I hid my head under the covers as Richard was hoisted out of bed and carried downstairs to the spanking and lecture that awaited him. His protestations that night haunt me to this day.

"But I didn't do anything." *WHACK!* "I didn't do anything." *WHACK!* "I didn't do anything." *WHACK!*

As Richard and I got older, sibling rivalry got so intense that we could no longer sleep in the same room at the same time. My father's method of discipline had to be updated as well. Rather than try to figure out whose fault it was—that is, which twin first provoked the other—Dad decided both of us would be punished. This was accomplished by placing one twin over his knee at a time and hitting us, only once, with a gun belt, which was as thick as three regular belts! *It got our attention.*

To further complicate my parents' bedtime dilemma, I would go to bed in their room, Richard in our room. After the evening news, my parents would take me, the sleeping child, upstairs to where my twin was already fast asleep. The bunk beds had long since been dismantled, and now the two beds were placed at opposite ends of our room. It all worked out rather well and nighttime spankings were quite rare . . . until one night when my mischievous streak reared its ugly head.

Late one evening I found myself awake. I noticed that Richard was restless and every half hour or so would get up to go to the bathroom. It was time to make my move. I decided to make up my bed as if I were still in it—to avert suspicion—and slide down one side of Richard's bed next to the wall. Barely visible, I would wait for my brother to return from his bathroom ritual.

Without hesitation, Richard plopped back into bed. I could hardly quiet my breathing as I remained hidden from view, ready to pounce on my unsuspecting victim. I waited a few minutes and then laid my right hand on his chest. My brother gasped but did not say a word. I began to move my hand ever so slowly up his chest toward his throat. Richard seemed paralyzed with fear. I could hear air being sucked into his mouth, as though he were gearing up for one big scream, but still nothing came out.

I continued my trek, moving my fingers like a large spider making its way toward prey. Just as my fingers neared his throat, the air that had been sucked in like a vacuum cleaner exploded from his lungs and mouth, filling the entire house with a tortured cry like a dog gone wild. Every attempt to calm him with the words "It's Michael, it's Michael" were in vain as he jumped out of bed and began running in circles wailing louder than before. I had never seen such a thing. I was amazed! Just then Dad burst through the door.

"What the heck is going on?!" he shouted at the top of his voice.

Even Richard didn't know quite what to say, still dazed as he was by my nighttime antics. In keeping with my father's new rule, both of us were spanked. I can still hear my brother pleading as if it were yesterday:

"But I didn't do anything." *WHACK!* "I didn't do anything." *WHACK!* "I didn't do anything." *WHACK!*

Now lest you think that I was overly cruel and took unfair advantage of my brother, let me assure you that our teen years seem to have evened the score. And so, another story comes to mind. In the fall of our seventh grade year in school, Richard and I were given an allowance that included enough money for a required monthly haircut. Richard persuaded me that if we could cut each other's hair, we could pocket the savings. There was only one catch: I had to go first.

The plan involved going to the upstairs bathroom and using our father's straight razor—with the door locked, of course. Running the razor carefully over my scalp, Richard began to remove large chunks of unwanted hair. Things seemed to be going better than expected and talk of saving a small fortune over the next year filled the room . . . until Richard's facial expression changed.

With a look of wonder and surprise—as though Richard could hardly believe his eyes—he began to mutter, "Oh, no. Oh, I, ah . . . Gosh, Michael, I'm sorry."

Not the kind of thing one wants to hear from a barber, especially a novice.

"What?" I asked. "What's the matter?"

"Oh, I'm *so* sorry."

"Sorry for *what?* Will you tell me what's going on?"

Before Richard could explain, I began to run my fingers slowly through my hair. Starting at my crown and sliding my hand down the back of my head, I could feel that something was missing. Not believing my own sense of touch, I grabbed up my mother's cosmetic mirror to survey the results. As the small, hand-held mirror reflected the back of my head onto the large bathroom mirror, a large gasp filled the air.

"Oh, no," I moaned. "It's gone. The hair on the back of my head, it's all gone."

Because this was the late '60s, when hair defined a man, my discovery proved worse than a face filled with zits. Immediately I began to cry.

"What am I going to do now?" I sobbed as Richard tried to comfort me. Of course, there was only one thing to do—tell Mom and Dad.

Certainly Mom and Dad would come to the rescue as they had always done in the past. They would know what to do.

Being compassionate parents of teens, they agreed that I could stay home from school for a day or two faking a not-so-serious head injury. Then for the next three months, I wore a bandage around my head to hide my pretend scar—giving my hair a chance to grow back. *Revenge for Richard had come at last!*

At this point, you may be asking yourself, "What does this have to do with teens who are doing well?"

Well, actually quite a lot. My experiences as a child and later as a young teen have caused me some concern as to how best to deal with my own son and daughter should history repeat itself. I can remember my mother frequently saying, "Wait till you have kids of your own." But I'm not waiting. While my kids are still young, I have decided—perhaps like many of you—to get a head start and look to the experts for wise counsel and advice. My search led me to the best—Dr. Nick Stinnett, who has devoted a lifetime of research to finding the principles and strategies of good parenting.

Nick explained to me that becoming a competent parent of successful teens did not come naturally, nor overnight. Parenting skills would need to be learned and practiced daily. Both of us agreed, however, that acquiring the skills necessary to raise whole and happy teens was simply not enough—parenting had to be *caught, not taught.* Nick told me that he had begun a national research project to identify high-wellness teens—that is, adolescents who are responsible, emotionally healthy, wise decision makers, and well-adjusted—so that all parents could learn from them. He was discovering what works for teens and why.

As our friendship developed, Nick and I cofounded an institute to raise funds to further the research. We have received support and cooperation from several universities including Abilene Christian University, Tennessee State University, Texas A&M University, and the University of Alabama.

The findings were exciting and caused us to think about how

unfortunate it is that such a widespread perception exists of adolescence being a typically unhappy, tumultuous, negative period of life. This pervasive perception has caused parents, like me, to dread and fear my children's teen years. Such pessimism about adolescence is greatly influenced by our own limited family experiences and by the fact that the media and social science research have focused almost exclusively on the problems and dysfunctional behaviors of today's teens.

Our research is different. It focuses on teenagers who are prospering and thriving in a holistic sense—socially, emotionally, physically, spiritually, and intellectually. We set out to search for the *secrets of high-wellness adolescents.* Across America we came in contact with many teens from age thirteen to nineteen, representing all levels of family income. They came from diverse racial and ethnic backgrounds. Many religious faiths were represented.

These adolescents talked to us through questionnaires and interviews. Teens from each of the fifty states gave us answers to many questions about their adolescent experience. The search brought together the insights and experiences of more than four thousand boys and girls who have a high degree of wellness.

In the following pages, we will outline and explain the secrets we found. We have shared them with others. We now want to share them with you.

And, oh yes, I would like you to know that both my twin and I turned out just fine. In fact, I'd like to leave you with one positive story from our past to help you begin your discovery of the secrets of high-wellness teens and to highlight the importance of looking at what's right versus what's wrong.

It was a hot summer evening, and my father and mother were watching TV. It was the kind of television program we kids didn't enjoy, so we were playing outside in the backyard. Billy, my oldest brother, was in his bedroom reading a book.

Our sister, Dee, a few years older than Richard and me, had joined us for a game of flashlight tag.

We were having fun racing around the yard. Eventually getting tired, we decided to take a break. Our house had a patio with chairs and a table, and it was there that we usually relaxed. Also on the patio that night was a large trunk that my father had brought home just a few days before. My mother liked antiques, and the old trunk would be a nice addition to her early American collection.

Walking over to the trunk with a flashlight, Richard opened the lid and began inspecting the interior.

"Hmmm," Richard pondered, "I wonder if this would be a good place to hide."

"Only one way to find out," Dee responded. She had Richard and I hold the lid open while she stepped into the trunk. "Whatever you do, don't close it," my sister cautioned as she curled up inside.

Richard stepped back to get his flashlight and asked me to continue holding up the lid. As he turned to walk away, the lid slipped from my grasp and, to my absolute horror, slammed down hard onto the base of the trunk, jamming the lock. I pulled and jiggled and twisted the lock, but it wouldn't budge. I was mortified.

Dee grew hysterical. "Get me out! Please! Get me out!"

About a year earlier, my father had told me that when someone is stuck in a closed environment, the first thing to do is make a small hole for air—so that's what I did! I quickly ran downstairs into our basement, got my father's chisel and hammer, and plopped down beside the trunk. As I began hammering the chisel into the roof of the trunk, my twin held the flashlight closely so I could see. In no time, a hole was made.

By then my father had joined us on the patio. Sizing up the situation, he grabbed the chisel and hammer from my hands and with one mighty blow, he broke the lock, which released the lid. My sister was free! What my father did next surprised us all. He pulled us close to him and, in one big bear hug, began to squeeze tightly. Instead of anger, my father displayed appreciation. He thanked my sister for not panicking, he thanked Richard for holding the light steady so I could see and staying with my sister when I went for tools, and he thanked me for acting quickly and remembering his words.

It was a close call. But we pulled together—*all of us!* Everyone helped. Yes, we were family and that evening we slept a bit more soundly and a bit more securely knowing that we were all under the same roof.

MICHAEL O'DONNELL
June 1996

ONE

The Odyssey

The letter arrived on a Monday morning. There was nothing to suggest that it was different from the usual correspondence. As the words on the paper were read, it quickly became clear that this was different.

> *I know you are doing research on adolescents and families. Maybe it will help a lot of people. I'm sorry to say it's too late to help me and my son.*
>
> *He changed so quickly. Maybe I had not been paying close enough attention. I noticed the change the most when he lost interest in school and his grades became just awful. He grew moody and I couldn't understand why. I couldn't talk with him anymore. He just drifted away from me.*
>
> *It was a year ago today as I write this letter to you that I came home from work and opened the door of my son's room to find the*

most unspeakable, devastating scene of my life. My son had shot himself.

I have nearly driven myself crazy with questions of "why?" and "what if . . ." I will probably never find the answer to those questions. But I do know he needed something he was not getting and I guess I was a big part of that. I know he was influenced too much by the wrong kind of group and wrong kind of values.

But I can't do anything about that now. The reason I am writing to you is to encourage you in your research and say thank you for spending your time this way. It is my hope and prayer that there can be more information about teenagers who are doing well and why they are doing well. It can help people to have this knowl-edge. We hear too much about the problems.

The words of this mother touched our hearts with sadness and compassion. We were filled with admiration that in the depths of her pain and loss she could reach out and think of helping others. Her letter also encouraged us.

There's Good News—and Bad

With the help of thousands of adolescents we have an excellent idea of what a high-wellness teen is and how wellness and health can be nurtured in adolescents. This book will become a very special possession for you. It offers a guide for how adolescents can experience the well-being, health, and happiness which teens and parents much desire.

Many teens across America *are* doing well. Because no one speaks for them and because the media focuses on those who are not doing well, little is known about high-wellness teens. This book is the medium through which the high-wellness adolescents speak to us about their lives and about what has been important in nurturing their health and wellness. This book is based upon research with four thousand adolescents across the nation who experience an optimal degree of wellness and health in the emotional, social, intellectual, and physical components of their lives. We thank these four thousand teens for their help. It is our sincere hope that their voices will be a help and a strength to the mother who wrote the letter, to all parents and teenagers, and to all people who work with adolescents.

Unfortunately, a recent Carnegie report on adolescents concluded there has been a substantial increase in serious social problems such as suicide, violence, and drug abuse among teens. The Carnegie report also indicated that many problems which were formerly experienced by older teens are now increasingly experienced by younger teens and that young teens are becoming much more at risk.[1]

As the mother who wrote the letter to us suggested, we hear so much about the problems of many teens that we often overlook the fact that many adolescents are doing well. Although this book is about high-wellness teens, perhaps it would help our perspective to first look at some teens who are not doing well.

He Is Only Sixteen

He is only sixteen. Cephus has shot and killed seven people. He has been shot himself four times. All of the killings and shootings have been over drugs.

Cephus said he didn't feel too bad about killing when he thought about the money he was making.

"After the first time," Cephus said, "I was kind of paranoid, but then I kind of started liking it.[2]

"I don't even have a place to live here. I just stay with different people," he shared. "I don't have a home and there ain't nobody to care if somebody did kill me.

"I ain't scared of getting killed," Cephus said. "I ain't got nothing to do, so I may as well get it over with and go to heaven or hell, but just get it over with."

Everything Is About Drugs

During the past eight years, eighteen-year-old Hoover has been kicked out of school twice. He has waged gun battles with rival gang members. He has broken into cars and houses.

"One time at 3 A.M., someone shot into my bedroom window," Hoover said, ". . . that bullet went all the way through the house and if I had been standing up, that bullet would have gone through my neck. . . . I looked out the window and saw the car driving away and then I got on the phone.

"The next night we were shooting into their house," he stated.

What causes most of the violence?

"Everything is about drugs," Hoover replied. "That's how they [gangs] get their money. They get geekers [addicts] to break into people's houses and steal so they can get money to buy the drugs."

The gangs give drugs to addicts as compensation for what they steal.

Rival gangs also steal drugs from each other, according to Hoover.

"I've seen a lot of people die or go to prison," Hoover said, "Just about all the older kids from my neighborhood are either dead or in prison."[3]

Sex and Violence

The following types of events are increasingly in the news and reflect a growing trend linking sex and violence:

• In Glen Ridge, New Jersey, twelve adolescent boys gathered in a basement room and watched as sexual acts were performed on a 17-year-old mentally retarded girl from their neighborhood. The girl was violated with a baseball bat, a stick, and a broom.

• In Fort Worth, Texas, a 13-year-old girl was held down by a half dozen boys ages 12 through 14 while another boy sexually assaulted her on a crowded school bus. Other students on the bus laughed as the girl was being assaulted.

• Eight high school students in a middle-class suburb of Los Angeles were accused of raping and molesting girls in a gang competition to accumulate "points" for their sexual conquests. The victims were 13, 15, and 16 years of age and one of the girls was 10 years old at the time of the incident.[4]

Unfortunately there are many stories similar to the ones you have just read. They are not happy stories, but they are important. They are important because they tell of the pain so many teens experience and because such stories mirror the condition of an entire society.

Enter the Art Gallery

Come and join us in a fantasy tour. We are visiting an art gallery. We walk together up the steps, open the gallery doors, and see before us many paintings. As we pause to look at the paintings, our happy anticipation turns to horror, depression, pessimism, and anxiety. An overwhelming sense of sadness and hopelessness begins to surround us.

Unfortunately, the contents of these paintings are not fantasy—they are real. We have seen them before, but we have chosen to turn away because what we see makes us uncomfortable.

But now we cannot turn away from the paintings in the gallery. We must continue our tour and consider what we see.

Each painting illustrates a message about how our adolescents in America are doing. We stop at the first painting and ponder its meaning.

• The typical adolescent takes in between 1,900 and 2,400 sex-related messages each year by television alone.

We move to the next several paintings.

• Teens are becoming sexually active with more partners at younger ages. Researchers at the Centers for Disease Control tell us that over 50 percent are sexually active by age seventeen.

• Many of those who begin sexual activity at an early age do not use any contraceptive method. Consequently, they are very apt to have an unintended pregnancy.

• The incidence of out-of-wedlock births to adolescent mothers has increased by 400 percent since 1955. In fact, the United States has the highest teen pregnancy rate of any developed country.

• As the Alan Guttmacher Institute reports, women who become mothers in their teens are four times more likely to find themselves living in poverty later in their lives than do those who become mothers after adolescence.

• Eating disorders have dramatically increased. Anorexia nervosa, for example, has more than doubled in the last twenty years.

• Since 1986, the number of youth killed by firearms rose 144 percent. American teens have become much more violent over the last forty years. Approximately 20 percent of all violent crimes are committed by youth under the age of eighteen. What we are seeing is a young, more violent juvenile offender, according to many law enforcement officers.

• The percentage of youth using drugs by the sixth grade has tripled over the last decade, and the use of marijuana among eighth graders has more than doubled since 1991.

• The use of inhalants by high school seniors has increased by nearly 50 percent since 1980.

Finally, the most horrifying painting of all!

• Suicide among adolescents has tripled during the last thirty years. It is the second leading cause of death among white teens and third among black youth. What is wrong in the world of adolescents that causes so many to lose hope and to feel that life is not worth living?

Other paintings remain which convey negative messages about adolescents. But we do not wish to remain at the art gallery any longer. It is too unpleasant.

We hurry toward the front doors of the gallery. As we are about to leave, the door to an adjoining room in the gallery swings open. A person holding that door open excitedly exclaims, "This room is filled with beautiful paintings. Come and see!"

As we walk into the adjoining room, we are immediately aware that the atmosphere is unclouded and refreshing. The beauty of these paintings captivates us. We see a panoramic view of robust, joyful adolescents.

The first painting that captures our attention portrays a glimpse in the life of a young woman who has successfully made the journey through her adolescence. She is beautiful and poised but cannot do something which most of us take for granted.

She Dances for God

She did not seem to realize she had won when Miss Virginia was announced as the first runner-up. When she became aware of what had happened, Heather Whitestone, Miss Alabama, began to cry and ducked her head to receive the crown of Miss America. She was crying and laughing as she walked down the runway. She signed "I love you" when she returned to the stage.

Heather lost all but 5 percent of her hearing after experiencing a bad reaction to a diphtheria-tetanus shot and a resulting high fever at age one and a half. She uses sign language and a hearing aid, and she reads lips.

Even though she cannot hear the music, Heather Whitestone enchanted the Miss America Pageant judges with her talent routine, a two-and-one-half-minute ballet performed to the song, "Via Dolorosa." When questioned about her dancing skills, Heather shares that the greatest help to her is that she keeps uppermost in her mind that she is dancing for God.

She has given much of her time to helping others, children and adults, to make goals, believe in themselves, and to hold and work toward achieving their dreams. She was involved in these activities before she became Miss America or Miss Alabama. She is a very positive, optimistic person with a genuine tranquillity that emanates from her. Her inner beauty shines in her eyes.

Many other beautiful paintings tell the stories of thousands of adolescents who are doing well. We invite you to join us on an odyssey to meet a part of America forgotten—successful, healthy teens. They are waiting to give you answers to the questions of what contributes to a happy, well-adjusted young person. They have a blueprint for what can work to bring about a good life in the teen years.

Their voices exclaim to us, "I am not that person addicted to drugs. I am not the rapist. I am not the killer.

"I am someone else and I want you to listen to me."

The Odyssey

We had just finished speaking at a conference in Ohio when a couple took us aside. There was an intensity and a kind of pleading in their eyes.

"We really need to talk with you," the mother began. "We have two children—a daughter who is fourteen and a son who is ten.

"We always considered ourselves to have a strong, happy family," she continued.

"This changed," the father added, "when our daughter became a teenager. She's surly and she always seems to be angry. She runs with a crowd that uses drugs. We're afraid she's using cocaine."

"Our lives have been turmoil," the mother said. "We want to turn this around. We want to help our daughter and we want to help our son avoid these problems and have a good teenage experience."

The father then asked, "Is there such a thing as a strong, cheerful adolescent?"

The mother quickly followed with another question, "What can we as parents do to rear a happy, healthy teenager?"

Those two questions echoed during the trip back from Ohio.

They were troublesome questions that many other parents had asked us. We began a search across the nation to find answers and came in contact with thousands of teens from diverse racial and ethnic backgrounds, all income levels, and most religious faiths.

The odyssey brought together the insights and experiences of these many adolescents who have a high degree of well-being. They have answered the two questions from the parents in Ohio as well as many other questions that you may have asked.

Here in the pages that follow are the answers to those questions. You are invited to share in the odyssey and hear their stories.

TWO

Cracking the Nut: Developing Good Problem-Solving Skills

. . . .

Today's teens must make more decisions and solve more problems than ever before. They are also confronted with these decisions and problems at earlier ages. These factors alone can create a great deal of stress. Yet because of the growing instability of families and increasing depersonalization of whole communities, there is less support for adolescents as they deal with the myriad decisions, problems, and stresses they face every day.

It is crucial that teens learn how to become *good* decision makers and problem solvers. This is one of the secrets of successful, healthy adolescents. Listen as four teenagers talk about the stresses they face:

"I get most stressed out when I'm pressured to make decisions I am not ready to make," said Sidney, a seventeen-year-old who lives in Los Angeles. "I have to decide about sending applications to colleges and trying to get scholarships. I'm being rushed into choosing what my college major will be, and I sort of feel like an oddball because I haven't made a career choice yet. My family wants me to be a medical doctor, but I don't think I want to do that. I don't really know *what* I want to do yet."

Ann, a fifteen-year-old from Colorado, said, "Two of my best friends snorted some cocaine at a party a few weeks ago. Since the party, they've both started buying it. They're really pushing me hard to try some."

Another fifteen-year-old, Andrew, plays high school football in Indiana. "Some of the guys in the locker room brag about their sexual conquests," he stated. "They tell all the details about how they scored with certain girls. They make you feel like you're not much of a man if you're not getting laid. This weekend they asked me to go with them to see a couple of prostitutes."

Antonio is thirteen years old and lives in New Jersey. "A lot of the kids in my town are in gangs," he said. "Some of my friends just joined a gang, and now they want me to come in. I don't know. Being a member gets you respect. The gang offers good protection, and there is strong friendship and loyalty in the gang. But . . . I know they do some bad things and once you're in, you're in for life."

Tough decisions, like those faced by Sidney, Ann, Andrew, and Antonio, also were experienced by the four thousand successful adolescents in our National Adolescent Wellness Research Project. Yet they have been successful in making the *right* choices. Making sound decisions and solving problems successfully were characteristic of the teens we talked to. Let's take a look at some other teenagers and their decisions—some of which were obviously poor choices, others which were wise. Then let's listen as some adolescents share their insights and strategies that helped them to do the right things.

Cool the Impulsiveness

It was an autumn night. A soft rain was falling on the mountain road over which Mark and his three friends were traveling. Mark was proud of his new Mustang GT, which his parents had given him as an early graduation present.

He looked at his watch. It was late—1:30 A.M.—and they still had fifty miles to go before reaching home. That was fine with Mark. They were having fun, and he certainly hadn't tired of driving his new car. He was pleased that he could make it "fly" when he wished.

Suddenly, a car that had been following them for a few minutes sped around them. As the car passed, the passengers taunted Mark with hand gestures. Taking the action as a challenge, he pushed the gas pedal to the floor. The speedometer quickly went to seventy-five miles per hour then to eighty-five. At ninety miles per hour, Mark began to pass the other car. The fast-approaching curve in the road was sharp, and Mark could not see around the bend. He felt himself losing control of the car. Then as he struggled to negotiate the curve, he looked directly into the lights of an oncoming truck.

The impact of the collision was ferocious. Pieces of the Mustang were found scattered as far as sixty yards from the point of impact. Mark's three friends and the driver of the truck were killed. Mark survived but lost the vision in his right eye.

Mark's anger and rash decision to pass the car brought a high cost for a little impulsive behavior. Obviously, this tragedy could have been avoided if Mark had controlled his temper and made the decision to let the other driver pass.

Impulsive behavior is often associated with bad judgment and hurried decisions, which usually only make matters worse. Research clearly indicates that juvenile delinquents tend to be far more impulsive than youths who are not delinquent. One of the most important qualities that contributes to successful problem-solving skills among the adolescents we talked to is their ability to avoid impulsive behavior. They have ways, they told us, of cooling their heels. The following story is one example.

Jake clenched his fists as the teacher stood in front of him and accused him of cheating. But Jake had not cheated. Another student sitting next to him had been whispering to him, trying to get answers. When Jake told him to stop asking for the answers, the teacher saw Jake responding and thought he was trying to cheat.

Feeling that his integrity had been called into question, Jake wanted to strike back. His first impulse was to yell at the teacher and tell her off. But he controlled his indignation. He took a deep breath and deliberately did not respond for several moments. He reminded himself that he needed to solve the problem, and a yelling match wouldn't accomplish that. Finally, when Jake spoke, he simply said, "I wasn't cheating. I know the material and will take another test if you want." The teacher was impressed by Jake's quiet but strong response to the situation, and the issue was soon resolved.

Looking Down the Road

Jennifer, a sixteen-year-old in Iowa, said, "I take my time making decisions. It's not smart to do the first thing that comes to mind without thinking through the situation. What helps me is looking down the road."

This important characteristic is evidenced among the successful teens we studied. These young people have learned the value of looking ahead and examining the potential consequences of their decisions and actions. This is in sharp contrast to the behavior of many troubled teenagers, who not only are very impulsive but also don't seem to consider the possible outcomes of their actions. Unfortunately, such shortsightedness can have long-term, and at times irreversible, consequences for their adult lives.

"I'm going to quit school," Juanita had said. "I can get a full-time job at a restaurant in town and make some money. Then I can afford to buy a lot of things I want.

"Besides," she had continued, "I don't like school much. It's a big bore. I think I'm really wasting my time when I could be working and earning money now."

Juanita, like too many others, did drop out of school. Her future job opportunities and potential income have been severely limited by her earlier decision not to get a high school education. Sadly, she had not looked down the road very far.

Compare Juanita's story with that of Roland. He could not afford expensive clothes or a car like many of his high school classmates. His parents made relatively low salaries and, like many parents, had a tough time simply paying the monthly bills and keeping food on the table.

"I wanted to go to college," Roland said, "but I knew my parents couldn't afford to send me. I was thinking seriously about this by the time I was in the ninth grade. I looked into my crystal ball and saw that my best chance of going to college was to make good grades and get a scholarship."

Roland worked toward his goal and studied hard. He succeeded in keeping his grades up, and he won a scholarship to the University of Nebraska. He reaped the positive consequences of his disciplined behavior. An important reason was that he was able to look ahead and see the potential benefits of choosing wisely to study hard and make good grades.

Taking Personal Responsibility

Monica's parents divorced when she was fifteen. When her dad
left, he told Monica, "I don't want any more responsibility for
this family. There will be no money from me for anyone, including you. I don't intend to spend one dime on your college
education. You're on your own!"

Monica, of course, was deeply hurt by the words and actions
of her father. The disappointment was bitter, but time helped
to heal the emotional wound somewhat. The family's financial
situation, however, grew even worse over time. Her father had
meant what he said—he cut off nearly all personal contact, and
absolutely all financial support. The family struggled to pay the
bills. Throughout high school Monica had to do without many
things which other teens take for granted.

During her senior year of high school, her mother remarried.
Nevertheless, the family income did not improve substantially,
and Monica's new stepfather could not provide any financial
support for her to attend college. Monica was indeed on her
own. She said, "I realized that if I went to college, I would have
to pay for it myself. I wanted to go to college very badly. I was
determined to go. My grades and entrance test scores were not
good enough to get a scholarship, so that left just one way to
accomplish my goal—I would have to work.

"I worked full time for a year," she continued, "and saved
enough money to pay for my first semester. It felt like a great
victory when I actually started that first semester. For the next
four years, I continually worked at two or three jobs, averaging
thirty to forty hours a week, and went to school full time."

Monica earned her college diploma. There were certainly
times when she became tired and discouraged, but she kept her
mind focused on her goal and did not give up.

Monica's story helps us understand one important reason

why our four thousand teens are good problem solvers—they take personal control and responsibility for dealing with their predicaments. Surely, if Monica had not assumed responsibility and taken charge of her situation, she would never have gone to college.

Persistence

It was not easy for Monica to work thirty to forty hours a week and go to school full time, too. She possesses another quality that contributes to the successful problem-solving skills common among the teens in our study. That quality is *persistence.* There is no substitute for it in dealing with a quandary.

"My grandmother was the person who helped me to develop persistence and determination," said Monica. "She would tell me to ask God for persistence and patience, and that if I hung in there long enough, the problem would usually get solved.

"I saw her live that principle in her own life, and she handled problems really well. I admired my grandmother and wanted to be like her."

Another teen, named Lawrence, also exhibited a great measure of persistence in dealing with a major problem in his life. Because of a serious overweight problem, he was mocked and ridiculed by several of his junior high school classmates in the Michigan community where he lived. Lawrence had always had problems with other kids teasing him, but it was worse in junior high. Resolving to overcome his weight problem, he became involved in exercise and diet programs. He soon began to play tennis. Imagine the courage it took for Lawrence to get out and play tennis among other kids.

He made himself do it, and he kept at it until everyone noticed that he had shed many pounds and was in excellent shape. By the time he graduated from high school, Lawrence had become an outstanding tennis player. His determination and persistence had helped him overcome a problem which had been a major source of pain most of his life.

Persistence—demonstrated so clearly by Monica and Lawrence—is the practice of continuing to pursue a task or problem and not quitting when the going gets tough. It means staying with something until it is finished. And it is one of the important reasons the teens in our study are good problem solvers.

Another example of someone who possesses this valuable quality is Jon. He was smaller than most of the opposing linemen he played against on the football field. He almost did not get a scholarship because the prevailing opinion among coaches was that he was too small to play college football. But one midwestern university decided to take a chance and offered him a scholarship.

"I was determined I would play," said Jon. "I put out a lot of extra effort to make up for my lack of size, and I put in extra hours on my own to practice techniques so I could become proficient in the skills."

He did indeed become proficient. He was a starting guard in his sophomore year. He quickly became known as one of the best linemen in college football despite his small size.

Then just as he reached the top of his game, Jon was confronted with another challenge. He sustained a serious knee injury during his junior year, and many thought he would never play football again. But Jon was determined to regain his earlier form. He persisted in therapy and strengthening exercises for his knee. Little by little, his knee became stronger and he had an outstanding season in his senior year.

Seeing Hardship As an Opportunity

Heather Whitestone was the first woman with a disability to be crowned Miss America. She lost her hearing because of a bacterial infection at age one and a half. She was asked how she would prefer to have her deafness described.

"I don't care what word they use because it's a fact," Heather said. "I am handicapped. I am disabled. I am deaf or hearing impaired or whatever. But I always viewed my deafness as an opportunity for creating."

What a great insight into successful problem solving! To look at a problem as an opportunity helps develop a positive attitude and approach from the very beginning.

The hardship of deafness was changed into an opportunity by Heather Whitestone. She developed the STARS program to help and encourage other young people to deal successfully with their problems. The STARS approach involves five components: having a positive attitude, believing in one's dreams, facing obstacles, working hard, and building a support team.

Angela, a New Hampshire teen, states, "I like to take the negatives in my life and turn them into positives. You know, it's a choice. I can build on the positive or I can dwell on the negative and be miserable."

Jean, a teen from Arizona, said, "I am not physically attractive, and I can't really do much about that. It used to bother me a lot. Finally, I decided I was not going to be unhappy the rest of my life about something I could not control. So I found a flattering hairstyle and learned some makeup techniques and then I concentrated on other things. I don't neglect my appearance, but I concentrate on making my personality beautiful, too. I have many interests. I love to travel, for example, and learn about other people and other countries.

"I have fun and friends. My life is good," she continued. "I think I have become a better person. I've learned a lot about life that some of my friends who are very physically attractive have not yet learned."

Jean is right. Sometimes there are things in our lives that we cannot change or control. But we can always control our attitudes and our reactions to problems. Setbacks and obstacles almost always offer an opportunity for us to develop a skill or to become a better person. Jean certainly did not enjoy feeling that she was unattractive, but she took that problem and seized the opportunity to develop a beautiful personality.

Monica, the young lady we mentioned earlier, took the opportunity to become a good financial manager when her father left the family and stopped all financial support. She learned how to make money and manage money in order to accomplish her goal of going to college. This financial problem with which Monica was confronted also helped her to develop character and inner strength and confidence in her ability to deal effectively with future problems in her life.

Fritz, a high school senior in Pennsylvania, is another example of someone who turned a crisis into an opportunity. He experienced the pain of losing his older sister to death in an automobile accident.

"I was very close to my sister," he recalled. "She had taken care of me all my life and was my best friend. Her death was the hardest thing I have ever faced. I felt so empty and sick."

Fritz said that one of the most helpful tools in dealing with his sister's death was the book *Man's Search for Meaning* by Viktor Frankl. "He was a German psychologist who was imprisoned in a concentration camp during World War Two," Fritz explained. "I was really impressed with the fact that many prisoners were so depressed and overcome by their plight that they lost the will to live and died. The part of that book that changed my life was reading about those prisoners who survived. They were the ones who focused their attention and efforts toward helping others. So I thought if prisoners in the concentration camps could create something positive out of the horrors they experienced, then I could do the same thing.

"I applied this to my life," continued Fritz, "and I began to volunteer in a Big Brother–type program. I am matched up with some younger boys in my town who don't have very good family situations. We go on outings—to the movies or to the park to play ball. I help them with homework or school projects. I try to be a good friend to them just like my sister was to me. I make a difference to them but the biggest difference is in me. My pain is less. I still miss my sister, but I smile when I remember her, now."

The Nutcracker Plan

One of the teenagers we talked to, named James, developed a strategy for solving problems that he called his "Nutcracker Plan," because "following the steps in the plan will crack any nut of a problem you have." The steps in this plan are essentially the same as those shared by the rest of our teens across America. In fact, the Nutcracker Plan has been used successfully by many people of all ages.

The four steps in the Nutcracker Plan will help anyone become a better decision maker and problem solver. We can understand why when we consider each of the steps.

1. **Identify the Problem.** It is much easier to solve a problem if you know what that problem actually is. Sometimes we complain, fret, and worry over symptoms or side issues and never deal with the actual problem.

"I don't like simply to react to situations," shared Nancy. "I prefer to step back and ask, 'All right now, what is the real problem here?' Then I can decide how to go about solving it."

2. Acknowledge and Express Feelings About the Problem.
"There are times when I need to talk about my problems with
someone I trust," said Sarah, a fourteen-year-old from Kansas.
"It helps because I usually end up seeing the whole situation
more clearly after I've talked about it."

It can be therapeutic when we simply admit that we are
angry or scared about a certain problem and that it is normal to
have those feelings. Acknowledging that we have strong emotions about a problem enables us to go on to the next step of
doing something to overcome it.

3. Explore the Alternatives. When making a decision or solving a problem, it is essential to know what alternatives you
have. Find out the facts about your particular difficulty in order
to identify the various courses of action that are available. Expert problem solvers recommend listing all the alternatives you
can think of—regardless of how silly or unworkable you may
think they are.

Ted, a California teen, said, "When I have a big decision to
make, I like to write the facts and my options on paper. This
helps me to think more clearly and makes the decision seem
more orderly."

Ted's idea of writing the facts and alternatives on paper has
another benefit. It gives him a sense of power and hope. People
who lack problem-solving skills often have what is called "tunnel vision." They see only one or two courses of action and are
not aware of other alternatives that are available. For example,
adolescents who attempt suicide often have tunnel vision and
cannot see what choices there are to help alleviate their distress.
On the other hand, seeing the choices listed gives a person
confidence and reassurance that something can be done about
the problem. The realization that there are usually several courses of action available is encouraging and empowering.

4. Evaluate the Alternatives. Once the alternatives are identified, a marvelous aid to sound decision making and problem solving is to evaluate each available option thoroughly. Analyzing the advantages and disadvantages of each course of action can bring the decision into sharper focus and also make the process easier.

Ted writes on paper the advantages and disadvantages of each alternative. He said, "When I write out the plusses and minuses of each of my options, it seems to give me a solid foundation for making a decision. When these are on paper, I can go back and study them."

Ways to Help Your Teen Succeed

1. Include your teenager in family decisions. Call the family together when major decisions must be made. Weigh the pros and cons, and look at the long-term outcomes of your decisions by making lists and discussing each one together. This establishes a pattern for your child to follow when he has tough choices to make and you aren't there to help him through the process.

2. Allow for relationships with other adults that are strong and encouraging. In a single-parent home, this is especially important. Sometimes another adult can be a mentor for a teen who has a specific interest or need, and the adult can help reinforce what the parent would want for that child. These types of relationships could be found in your church or in community organizations, such as Big Brothers and Big Sisters, and Boy Scouts and Girl Scouts.

3. Be open and available for conversation and activities with your teens. When your child seeks your opinions, do all you can to follow through on the request. Avoid lecturing or jumping to conclusions. Your teen may ask, "When you were my age, did teens drink?" to find help in making a decision about drinking—*not* because she is already drinking. Learn to ask your child, "What do you think?," and then listen to the reply. This helps children to clarify their thoughts and to learn how to make decisions.

4. Provide opportunities for your teenager to be involved with other teens who have similar interests and values. Positive, enriching relationships with peers will go a long way toward reinforcing wise, responsible behavior for your child. Young people often learn the most from each other (both good and bad), so foster your teen's friendships with others who will provide support and prudent decision making. Encourage your teen to participate in your church's youth group, 4-H clubs, scouting, YMCA, or YWCA.

5. Encourage your teen to be involved in volunteer work at your church or in your community. This might mean extra hours on your part to drive your child to and from activities, but the time and effort will be well worth it. Your relationship with your teen might be strengthened by doing this work together. Be sure to let teens choose the activities that have interest for them.

Tips for Teens Who Want to Succeed

1. When you feel overwhelmed or stressed, take time out to look at all of your options. You might get a piece of paper out and write down all your options and think about the pros and cons for each one. Think about what will happen if you act on the choices that you have written. Also, seek the opinions of people you respect and bounce the ideas off of them.

2. Set goals for yourself. Where do you want to be a year from now? Five years from now? Ten years from now? Decide what you will have to do to reach the goals you have set. Make a plan for how you will achieve your goal.

3. Look for adults you respect and build relationships with them. You can learn a lot by observing those who have more life experience than you and are willing to share the lessons they have learned.

4. Start making friends with other teens who have similar goals and values and who will help encourage you to meet your goals. You might think about joining a group such as 4-H, Boy Scouts or Girl Scouts, Junior Achievement, school clubs, or local sports teams.

5. Get involved with your church's youth group. Surrounding yourself with like-minded peers is a great way to reinforce wise decision-making skills. And you can help others to learn the valuable skills outlined in this chapter.

6. Do volunteer work for your church or for your community. You could assist in the church nursery or help with Bible classes for the children. You might be involved with homeless shelters or soup kitchens, organizations such as Meals on Wheels or the Red Cross, a food bank, or recycling.

7. Learn some techniques to curb impulsive behavior. When you feel angry, count to ten or recite "Be cool, be cool, be cool" before you act. Ask yourself, "Will this hurt someone?" "Will this hurt me?" "Will I wish I hadn't done it?" If you have doubts, delay doing anything for a few hours or days.

How Can I . . . ?

1. List some of the problems, obstacles, or challenges facing you. What are opportunities that each presents? Be creative. Be optimistic. Use your sense of humor.

E X A M P L E

Problems/Challenges
Must work to have spending money

Opportunities
Greater independence
Work experience
Meet people at work

2. Practice the steps in the Nutcracker Plan. *Identify the problem.* Write down each person's ideas. Eliminate side issues; focus on the root or base problem. If you discover that you have two or three problems, separate them and deal with each independently.

E X A M P L E

Mom: *Susie spends lots of time alone in her room, seems depressed, sullen. She is increasingly rebellious.*
Susie: *Mom spends all her time with her friends. She doesn't care about me. Why should I care about her?*

Problems: lack of communication, rebellion. *Acknowledge and Express Feelings About the Problem.* Identify feelings associated with the situation. Allow feelings. Do not judge: "You shouldn't feel that way." Do not defend: "I didn't mean. . . ." Listen with your heart as well as ears.

E X A M P L E

Mom fears *that Susie is shutting her out. She is* worried *about depression. She is* hurt *by the rebellion and the closed door.*
Susie feels abandoned *when Mom is gone so much. She is* lonely *and* sad *and* angry.

Explore the alternatives. Write all options—from the very sensible on. Do not evaluate them now.

E X A M P L E :

Options to improve communication:
Do nothing, learn to live with it.
Professional counseling for Susie, for Mom, together.
Cooperative attitude by Susie rewarded (special outing with Mom, car privilege).
Two evenings each week for Mom and Susie to talk, shop, etc. together.
Mom stops seeing her friends.
Susie is punished for rebellion (grounding, loss of TV time).

Evaluate the Alternatives. Which is most easily done? What is the cost (money, time, energy) involved with each? What is most apt to be effective?

E X A M P L E

Doing nothing is not acceptable. Mom needs to have friends. Mom and Susie can spend two evenings together simply by agreeing on the days. They can shop, cook, go to a movie, talk, etc. They would prefer to reward Susie's cooperative behavior. She is eager to earn some car privileges. If the situation (especially the depression) does not improve in one month, they will seek professional help.

THREE

Roots and Wings:
Strong Families

· ·

Many adults mistakenly believe that conflict and hostility between parents and their teen children are inevitable. They reason that parents should become uninvolved or detached from teens in order to encourage their adolescents to become independent. Many families and teens, however, have demonstrated that conflict and hostility can be overcome and that close, warm relationships can be maintained.

Contrary to what we often hear, adolescents want to have good relationships with their parents. They need close associations with caring adults who are committed to them. We were not surprised, then, that the four thousand high-wellness adolescents in the National Adolescent Wellness Research Project told us that a strong family (in all forms—two parent, single parent, stepparent, or grandparent-headed) was one of the major reasons their adolescence has been a positive, happy experience. In contrast, when adolescents characterized by a low degree of wellness were asked what were the major reasons their adolescence has been a negative, unhappy experience, their most common reply was "family problems."

In another study of adolescents, the Carnegie Council concluded that teens develop best when they have a warm, supportive family environment characterized by a sustained parental interest in and responsiveness to their lives.[1] Our National Adolescent Wellness research causes us to agree with the conclusion of the Carnegie report and indicates that a close, supportive family atmosphere provides powerful protection against the risks of becoming involved in unhealthy, antisocial behavior. Strong, caring families give adolescents the "roots and wings" they need for successful, healthy lives.

The adolescents in our study who had the highest degree of wellness were in a nuclear family structure where both parents were present and both parents were the parents of the children in the home. These youngsters described their family relationships as close and positive. Their families possessed six strengths that have made a major contribution, perhaps the most important contribution, to the teens' well-being and health.

Through these six qualities the strong families, in all their forms, have provided a sense of belonging, guidance, love, self-esteem, confidence, and purpose. They have given their adolescents roots and wings.

Communication

The lifeblood of any relationship is communication—free and honest sharing of thoughts and feelings between two or more people. In numerous surveys, teens describe one of their most important needs as someone with whom they can talk. They need someone who will listen to them. They need to have meaningful communion of thoughts and feelings with someone who cares. The successful teens experience that type of communication in their families.

"One thing I really appreciate about my parents," said a South Dakota teen, "is that they really listen. They are always there for me to talk with them about anything."

How many people do you know who truly listen? Our society does not do a very good job of helping people learn how to listen or to learn the importance of listening. Many of us go about our daily lives asserting our wishes, talking about things that interest us, and pursuing our individual goals but spending little or no time listening to others. The result? Others perceive (and accurately) that we do not understand them or care about them. This is exactly the way teens feel when no one in the family listens to them. In our survey of teens, we found that one of the greatest needs they felt was the need to have someone with whom they could talk at a deep level.

Ron, a teenager from Washington state, said, "I hope I can become as good a listener as my parents. My parents are expert listeners and that is one very important reason why our relationship is good. When someone listens to you, they show respect and true interest. You must have both of those things in your life."

Those words from Ron—"when someone listens to you, they show respect and true interest"—should be stamped on the dining-room tables of every home in America. Successful adolescents spend much time talking with the members of their families. This keeps the family communication channels open and helps to build solid relationships.

Delores, a New Jersey teen, states, "My family talks with each other about all kinds of things. I mean, we talk about some pretty heavy, personal stuff. But you know, a lot of our conversation is about the news, sports, work, or just trivial matters. We simply enjoy talking with each other."

Did the families of the healthy adolescents experience conflict? Of course they did! The important difference was the way these families dealt with conflict.

Reese, a sixteen-year-old from Tennessee, said, "We have disagreements in my family, and we have some very emotional arguments. But we have a rule about arguments: We don't attack one another or tear each other down. We focus on solving the problem. We honestly try to resolve the conflict to meet everyone's needs as much as possible."

Andrea, a teen from New Mexico, said, "Whenever we have conflicts, I'm always encouraged to express my feelings. Everyone's voice is heard. I think this practice has helped our family deal with disagreements successfully."

So the families of the high-wellness teens deal effectively with conflict by following certain important principles. They focus their attention on solving problems. They avoid attacking each other and tearing each other down. All of the family members are encouraged to express their feelings about the situation. Other practices that help them to deal capably with conflict include identifying all of the alternative options and methods for resolving the disagreement, evaluating the advantages and disadvantages of each option, and then choosing the one that seems to be the best for everyone.

Time Together

Time spent together was a crucial ingredient for strong family relationships among the adolescents we studied.

"We do everything together," said Joel, from Montana. "We do chores together, eat together, take trips together, and go hunting and rafting together."

"It's not forced togetherness," remarked sixteen-year-old Joan, who lives in Maine. "We really enjoy being together. I think being together a lot helps us to communicate better and understand each other more."

We recently asked a sample of older adolescents the question, "How did your father show you that he loved you while you were growing up?" One teenager gave an answer that saddened us especially because it represented the same feelings that several others reported. He said, "My father didn't. He never knew me well enough or spent enough time with me to show that he loved me!"

What a sad commentary. This lack of time and involvement is not limited to fathers; mothers are sometimes absent as well. And this problem plagues thousands of families at every income level. Many marriage and family therapists believe that the major problem facing families today is insufficient time together.

In these modern times, the situation in many families is that both parents must work to provide basic necessities. Although many are successful in balancing the demands of work and home, the result for other families is that they spend so little time together that their ability to communicate wanes. Family members are unaware of what is going on in the hearts and minds of one another because they are simply not with each other enough to know. These disconnected families fail to develop a sense of unity and identity. They're not a family in a complete sense; they're just a bunch of people living under the same roof.

Adolescents desperately need the most precious gift their families can give—time. Tragically, many never received that gift as children and will not receive it as adolescents. The consequences are grave and may be transmitted from generation to generation. This principle is well illustrated by the song "Cat's in the Cradle" by Harry Chapin.

CAT'S IN THE CRADLE

My child arrived just the other day;
he came into the world in the usual way.
But there were planes to catch and bills to pay;
he learned to walk while I was away.
And he was talkin' 'fore I knew it,
and as he grew he'd say,
"I'm gonna be like you, Dad,
you know I'm gonna be like you."

And the cat's in the cradle and the silver spoon,
little boy blue and the man in the moon.
"When you comin' home, Dad?" "I don't know when,
but we'll get together then;
you know we'll have a good time then."

My son turned ten just the other day;
he said, "Thanks for the ball, Dad,
come on, let's play.
Can you teach me to throw?"
I said, "Not today,
I got a lot to do."
He said, "That's okay."
And he walked away,
but his smile never dimmed.
He said, "I'm gonna be like him, yeah,
you know I'm gonna be like him."

And the cat's in the cradle and the silver spoon,
little boy blue and the man in the moon.
"When you comin' home, Dad?" "I don't know when,
but we'll get together then;
you know we'll have a good time then."

Well, he came from college just the other day;
so much like a man I just had to say,

"Son, I'm proud of you, can you sit for a while?"
He shook his head and he said with a smile,
"What I'd really like, Dad, is to borrow the car keys;
see you later, can I have them, please?"

And the cat's in the cradle and the silver spoon,
little boy blue and the man in the moon.
"When you comin' home, Dad?" "I don't know when,
but we'll get together then;
you know we'll have a good time then."

I've long since retired, my son's moved away;
I called him up just the other day.
I said, "I'd like to see you if you don't mind."
He said, "I'd love to, Dad, if I can find the time.
You see, my new job's a hassle and the kids have the flu,
but it's sure nice talkin' to you, Dad,
it's been sure nice talkin' to you."
And as I hung up the phone, it occurred to me,
he'd grown up just like me;
my boy was just like me.

And the cat's in the cradle and the silver spoon,
little boy blue and the man in the moon.
"When you comin' home, Dad?" "I don't know when,
but we'll get together then;
you know we'll have a good time then."

Traditions were reported by the successful adolescents in our study as being a very important component of spending time together as a family. Family traditions have great power to fortify the bonds of relationships within a family. Cultivating traditions is too often ignored as a strategy for strengthening families and specifically for strengthening parent-adolescent relationships, because traditions take time and effort. They are well worth the time and effort, however, according to those surveyed for our National Adolescent Wellness Research Project.

Traditions are the "we always" activities—such as "we always have pancakes on Saturday mornings" or "we always celebrate birthdays with a special dinner and fun outing." They may occur once a day, once a week, once a month, or once a year. Whatever the frequency, however, traditions happen regularly and consistently.

"We always play cards every Friday night," said one Texas teen. "I look forward to the games each week. They're fun. We have popcorn and talk while we play. It's a time when we can catch up with each other."

One Michigan adolescent shared, "One tradition in my family that some people might think is strange is reading books aloud together. We all agree on the book that's selected, and we take turns reading to each other. We usually do this a couple of nights a week and always when we have to take long trips by car. I really enjoy this reading time together. Mysteries or ghost stories are my favorites."

Melissa, an eighteen-year-old from Georgia, told about one of her favorite family rituals. "My grandmother lives on a farm," she said, "and for as long as I can remember, we've gone there for Thanksgiving. Grandma gives each child a paper sack and sends the children off to the pecan grove for the 'Great Pecan Picking Contest.' Grandma gives a special prize to the one who picks the most pecans. Well, actually, she gives everyone a prize. She's smart—she started a family tradition that was fun and it was a good way to get her pecans picked, too.

"You know, it's funny," Melissa continued, "I still look forward to going there at Thanksgiving to pick those pecans."

Commitment

The families of the adolescents possessing a high degree of wellness shared a special kind of love—a love that does not change with mood swings, hard times, or the passage of years. It is a love that is conscious and unconditional. It says, "I decide and promise to love you because of who you are, not because of what you do or how I feel."

Commitment love is the glue that holds all of the other family strengths together. Four thousand sound adolescents described it in many different ways, but the importance of it in their lives was unmistakable.

"It is a fierce loyalty," said one Arkansas teenager. "I know my family is for me a hundred percent, and they'll stand by me no matter what. There's great security in that feeling."

For two years, seventeen-year-old John M. suffered a malady that afflicts thousands of adolescents—depression. "It affected everything I did," he recalled. "I would feel so miserable sometimes that I would not want to go on living. I usually didn't even know why I felt so bad. Sometimes I couldn't concentrate on anything."

John's depression became so severe that at one point he had to be hospitalized. "I remember lying in the hospital bed and my dad holding my hand, telling me he loved me, and everything would be all right."

Physicians finally diagnosed a physical cause for John's depression and prescribed therapy treatments for a chemical imbalance. Today, John is free of the depression that had been so debilitating at times.

"The doctors were important, and I'm thankful for them," John said. "But there is no question in my mind that I would not have gotten through the depression without the love of my family. They were there for me. They were patient when I was at my worst. They loved me when I wasn't lovable. That commitment will carry with me the rest of my life."

Commitment such as this has great power because it affirms the worth of a person's life and communicates unconditional regard for that person. This creates an interpersonal environment that nurtures self-esteem, a sense of roots and belonging, security, and a capacity to love.

Commitment was reflected in the families of these adolescents in another way—a commitment to the family group. These families had decided to make the family a top priority with respect to the way members invested their time and energy.

A common plague of modern life is that family members find themselves overextended and fragmented. Their lives are pulled in a thousand different directions, leaving them with only leftover time for one another. When they are together, they are worn out from the rest of life, too tired and too distracted to focus on each other.

Do the strong families of the successful adolescents face the same demands and time scarcity of daily life as everyone else? Of course they do! It is how they deal with this challenge that is a demonstration of their commitment to the family group.

"When life gets to be too much of a hassle," shared fifteen-year-old Charles, "our family has a routine that works. The whole family sits down and talks about everything each person is involved in. It helps when we write down everything on a piece of paper. We usually can't believe that we are really doing all this stuff, and agree that we're doing too much.

"Each one of us goes over his individual list," Charles continued, "and we drop off those involvements that either are not necessary, that we don't really enjoy, or that are simply not important. This keeps more sanity in our lives, and it certainly gives us more time together as a family."

This practice was typical of the way these families prevented the hassles and "busyness" of daily life from minimizing their relationships. It is a powerful example of how they made their families a priority. By periodically reviewing their involvements and crossing some off their list, these families accomplished two important purposes. First, they freed up time to spend together as a family in a more relaxed, less hurried, and less fragmented atmosphere. Second, they reduced a substantial amount of stress from the family as a whole and also for individual members.

Appreciation

The adolescents included in our research reported that their families express a great deal of appreciation to each other. They give each other many sincere compliments. They build up one another's self-esteem and confidence. They make each other feel good about themselves. By engaging in such behavior, these families help to satisfy one of the most important needs in the lives of their adolescent members.

William James, a pioneer in the field of psychology, published a book on human needs. A few years after it was published, he remarked that he had failed to include what he considered the most important need of all—the need to be appreciated.[2]

Numerous studies have shown that workers in offices, factories, schools, and elsewhere want one thing more than anything else—appreciation. Do you agree? Ask yourself why you work so hard. Money is certainly an important motivation, and we all like to accumulate things in our lives. But few things that we own are so satisfying that we would want to wear ourselves out for them. Much of the time, appreciation is really what we are after. We want to be valued for who we are and what we do.

We want people to recognize our efforts and our accomplishments.

The expression of appreciation dominates the relationships of the families of healthy adolescents. Here are a few examples of what teens told us:

"My dad always tells my mom how pretty her dress is or how much he enjoyed a meal she prepared. He makes her feel very special."

"My parents don't harp on what I do wrong. They forget my mistakes. They remember the things I have done well. When I forget the good things I've done, they remind me."

"My parents always recognize me for my accomplishments at school or in sports. They make sure my grandparents know, too."

"We tell each other 'I love you' every night before going to bed. It gives me a cozy feeling. It also is reassuring to know that we care, and are pulling for each other."

"My mother thanks me for the little things I do. When I do chores around the house, she lets me know that it really helps. That makes me feel needed."

"I learned to show appreciation to other people mainly from the example of parents. They always express their gratitude to each other and me. From an early age they encouraged me to write thank-you notes and to tell others how much I enjoyed something they had done for me. The ability to express appreciation has made my relationships better."

From these families we have learned an important quality— the expression of appreciation, which helps their adolescents to grow and flourish as their self-esteem is enhanced. This in turn enables adolescents to show appreciation to others and enhance the quality of their relationships.

When we are appreciated by others, our self-esteem is increased and, as psychologist Don Clifton told us, we are getting our "self-esteem bucket" filled. But this bucket can easily tip over and is harder to fill than it is to empty. "If somebody puts you down," Clifton says, "they've got their dipper in your bucket. By my estimate, it takes about ten positive strokes to repair the damage of one negative."

Many people have bucket and dipper problems. Many husbands and wives can't seem to say anything good about each other. Parents criticize and belittle their children, who in turn complain about their parents.

The families of the strong adolescents have learned to fill their self-esteem buckets and in so doing give them a valuable resource for life. These adolescents learn to fill the self-esteem buckets of others, and they are more capable of doing so because their own buckets are full. Consider the thoughts that Pablo Casals expressed concerning what we teach children:

Each second we live is a new and unique moment of the universe, a moment that never was before and never will be again. And what do we teach our children in school? We teach them that two and two make four, and that Paris is the capital of France. Will we also teach them what they are? We should say to each of them, "Do you know what you are? You are a marvel. You are unique. In all of the world, there is no other exactly like you."[3]

Perhaps the adolescents in the National Adolescent Wellness Research Project have learned to view themselves and others in the manner that Pablo Casals described. This is one result of learning the art of appreciation.

Dealing with Crisis in a Positive Way

The basketball game was close and exciting as was expected when these cross-town rivals played each other. This particular game was more riveting than usual because the two teams were among the top high school women's teams in the state.

As the clock wound down, the winning basket was made by Rhonda, a tall, red-haired junior. The gymnasium erupted in wild cheers for the school's heroine.

Rhonda was ecstatic that she was able to help her team win. She loved basketball and was regarded as one of the most outstanding players in her region of the country. That she would receive a scholarship to play for a university was a foregone conclusion among the sports media, even though she was only a junior.

Two hours after sinking the winning basket, she left the school campus feeling on top of the world. It was indeed a special night. She didn't know then that it would be the last time she would play in a basketball game.

Rhonda and a couple of her teammates celebrated the victory together. They stopped to pick up a pizza and then headed for one of the girls' homes. The city lights began to fade as Rhonda picked up speed on the empty country road. She entered the curve too fast. Tires screeched on the pavement; the car slid and spun for what seemed like an eternity. Then it went off the road and rolled twice.

It was some time before a car passed by. Rhonda's two friends stood on the side of the road, frantically flagging down the approaching car. They were cut and bruised. One had a broken arm. Rhonda, however, didn't fare so well. She lay in the crumpled car unable to move.

When the ambulance arrived and paramedics moved her out of the car, Rhonda knew something was terribly wrong. She could not feel them moving her legs. In fact, she could feel nothing in the lower part of her body.

Days later, Rhonda looked with disbelief and shock into the eyes of the doctor who sat beside her bed and quietly told her she was paralyzed. The prognosis was that she would probably never walk again.

"It certainly wasn't easy for me to accept being bound to a wheelchair for life," Rhonda said. "I cried until I could cry no more. I was very angry. I think I've passed through the worst of the adjustment.

"I don't think I could have gotten through this without my family," she continued. "They have been the biggest help to me throughout the ordeal. They cried with me, and I knew they cared. They gave me hope and helped me see the bright side of things. They listened when I needed to talk. My dad in particular helped bring a little happiness to the dark days. He always got me to play board games or cards. He also bought me joke books, and we would read them together. It made me laugh, which I needed."

There were many reasons for Rhonda to remain devastated and to lose hope. It would have been understandable if she had developed a nasty attitude toward life. But she didn't. Her friends and neighbors have been surprised that she is remarkably upbeat. Some have asked, "How can she be so positive? Why isn't she completely depressed?"

Rhonda answers by saying, "Sure, there are plenty of things to feel bad about. But it doesn't do any good for me to dwell on those things. If I did, I'd feel worse. I have learned to look for the positive side of any problem."

She said that focusing on the positives—no matter how small—has helped her through the tough times. "There are some silver linings to this black cloud," she said. "I have more time to read, which I enjoy. I also can give more attention to people and relationships. Perhaps best of all, our family has become closer. Since the accident, we have all slowed down and we spend more time with each other. We don't seem to be nearly as rushed as we used to be. I think we enjoy our time together more now because we know how precious life is."

Rhonda's story illustrates two important reasons the families of successful adolescents are able to cope with crises and hard times. They are typical of the principles that helped these families to protect themselves from being destroyed by crises and to strengthen their bonds with each other.

First, strong families unite and help each other deal with troubles and difficulties. They consolidate their respective problem-solving skills and attack the issue together. They provide a good support system for each other. These families do not leave one member to handle the crisis alone. Their loyalty and support for each other are bolstered in tough times.

Second, these families have the ability to see something positive in a bad situation, no matter how tragic or bleak. This ability to see something good in a bad situation has a powerful influence on each individual family member's mental outlook and emotional stability. Identifying the positives in a crisis helps the family members realize they have resources and strengths from which to draw. Acknowledging the resources they possess increases the confidence that they can successfully deal with the crisis. Finding good things even in the worst situations provides adolescents with a balanced perspective of life.

Spiritual Wellness

The spiritual dimension is one of the most important secrets of success and strength for families and their adolescent members. These strong families describe their spiritual lives in various ways, including faith in God, a deep sense of purpose in life, concern for others, ethical and moral behavior, and a sense of unity with all living things.

Spiritual wellness is a unifying force for families, providing a solid core of love, care, and compassion for others. Questions concerning purpose and meaning in life are most often answered through spiritual pursuits. Spirituality is a force that helps an individual transcend self and become part of something larger.

"My older brother, Jordan, had a long streak of bad luck and couldn't get his life straightened out," said Ted, a West Virginia teen. "He was depressed and felt like a failure. He took drugs and alcohol to try to feel better. But that only made things worse. It seemed that everything he tried went wrong. When he was eighteen, he attempted suicide.

"My brother's problem was that he didn't have a reason to live," Ted continued. "He tried to find happiness by getting things and being popular, but that was empty. He had no hope that his life could get better. One night my dad sat down with Jordan and said, 'I know you feel hopeless and you feel like you don't have it in you to deal with your problems. But you *do* have something very powerful inside you. That power is God.'"

Jordan said that he believed in God, but didn't really feel His presence inside of him.

"My father told him that was his main problem," Ted continued. "Jordan needed to feel the presence of God in his life. He said that God was much bigger than his struggles. I'll never forget my dad's words: 'Jordan, God can heal you and make your life full and happy. Get to know that great, loving God and get caught up in something bigger than yourself.'"

Jordan acknowledged that he had made a mess of things by trying to handle everything on his own. And then he began crying.

"My brother had a spiritual experience that night," Ted said. "He told me that he surrendered control of his life to God and when he did, he felt a great relief and a change beginning."

Ted's brother continued to have some rough times. His problems didn't disappear overnight. But he gradually improved, and his depression lifted considerably. He began to study the

Scriptures, to meditate and pray. He attended worship services at a small church and soon was active in their food pantry program. His renewed spiritual commitment not only gave him hope and guidance, but also a deep sense of purpose and meaning in life.

"My brother found a reason to live that went far beyond money and social approval," Ted commented. "He's also now a volunteer at the drug rehab program in our community, and he knows he's doing something to help people."

The families like Ted's that have a solid spiritual foundation find practical, personal help for daily living. These families have a source of power to draw upon and a bond that holds them together. Their faith also provides them with a sense of being part of something larger than themselves. This in turn helps members to be less self-centered and to be more considerate of others.

Many strong family members have their spiritual wellness founded in the practice of their religious beliefs. They may express their spiritual dimension through affiliation with a church or synagogue, in prayer, and service to others. Members of some strong families have other ways of expressing their spiritual nature. They may devote themselves to helping humanity through efforts to eradicate hunger, poverty, child maltreatment, prejudice, hatred, and war. They may labor for the environment or the homeless. They may meditate on the beauty of nature or art or poetry. Whatever its source or expression, spiritual wellness is another resource that strong families provide for their adolescents. It is a resource that gives young people guidance in life and contributes significantly to their overall health and well-being.

Ways to Help Your Teen Succeed

1. **Cultivate good communication with your teen.** Start by thinking about how you talk with your teen. Are there times when you and your child throw up your hands and walk away from each other? Are there things that you have said and done that stopped a discussion? Decide to speak in encouraging ways to your teen. When saying things that are difficult, express your love and appreciation. Make a commitment to stay in verbal contact with your teen every day.

2. **Plan for regular family times.** Tell your teen and the other children in your home that they are important, and you are committed to spending time together as a family. Then follow through! Consistency is the key. Your kids will watch to see the kind of commitment you have. Some families set aside one night a week for family night: popcorn and movies (rented) or cards or crafts. Have a family outing every other month: picnic, camp, hike, take in a concert or craft fair.

3. **Maintain family traditions.** If some of your family traditions are falling by the wayside, take action. Renew the traditions and keep them going. Ask your children what traditions they appreciate and want to continue. Also, start new regular activities that might become traditions.

4. **Catch your son or daughter doing something good.** Part of appreciating your teen is recognizing his or her positive qualities and actions, and then praising them. Don't focus so much on the bad things that you overlook all the good things. If you are feeling particularly negative, ask a friend to be your sounding board and timer. Spend five minutes talking to that friend

about your teen—but you may only tell good things, why you are proud of your teen, and positive qualities of that child.

5. Look for the good in each crisis, and celebrate what is going right. What do you do when bad things happen? Do the members of your family pull together, or are they torn apart? Make an effort to be encouraging and supportive during tough times.

6. Examine the focus of your life. What is your reason for getting out of bed each morning? Who or what has control over your words, actions, and thoughts? Tell your teens about your motivations and passions in life. Share your spiritual side with your children.

Tips for Teens Who Want to Succeed

1. Stay open with your parents, even when it feels as though they don't understand. Communication takes work, and many times it's frustrating. But try to remain open and honest with your parents. Allow your parents to make mistakes, and try not to be easily offended. Initiate conversation about all sorts of things that are going on in your life. Don't wait for your parents or siblings to start a conversation.

2. Spend time with your family. Friends, work, school, and dating are important, but don't crowd your family out of your schedule. Have a positive attitude when your parents suggest that you do something together. Offer your own ideas for family times.

3. Help to maintain family traditions. If you see a tradition falling away, remind your parents about it and tell them that you want it to continue. Also, help to come up with new traditions that you think would draw your family closer together.

4. Tell your family members that you appreciate them. Thank your mom and dad for working to provide for you. Thank your aunt for driving you and your friends to the mall. Thank your grandmother for having your friends stay for dinner. See how many ways you can express your gratitude to your family.

5. In the middle of hard times, look for good things. Be a positive influence by helping and encouraging others. Without being phony or insincere, look for "silver linings" to the dark clouds and remind others of them. Good feelings tend to spread from person to person—so you be the one who starts them moving.

6. Cultivate your spiritual life. If you are searching for direction and meaning in life, talk to your parents or a trusted adult. Ask them about their beliefs and focus in life. Spend time in contemplation.

How Can I . . . ?

Put an "S" for *Strength* beside the qualities you feel your family does well. Put a "G" for *Growth* beside the qualities you feel need improvement. This exercise can help you to celebrate your achievements as well as to plan for growth.

Appreciation and Affection

_____kindness for each other

_____tolerance for differences

_____physical and emotional affection (hugs; "I love you")

_____enhance each other's self-esteem

_____feelings of security and safety

Commitment

_____honesty

_____"we are one"

_____sacrifice for each other and family

_____dependability

_____family identity

Positive Communication

_____open, straightforward

_____disagreements resolved soon

_____cooperative not competitive

_____nonblaming

_____discussion rather than lecture

Time Together

_____enjoy each other's company

_____unplanned, spontaneous good times

_____quality time in great quantity

_____simple, inexpensive good times

_____work together (chores, projects)

Spiritual Well-Being

_____good mental health

_____religious beliefs or ethical values which guide family

_____relationship with a higher power

_____oneness with humankind

_____network of friends, extended family

Ability to Cope with Stress and Crises

_____sharing feelings and resources

_____patience

_____resilience; ability to "hang in there"

_____understanding each other

_____ability to see "silver lining" or some good

FOUR

Fight or Flight: Managing Stress

S tress is one of the most destructive maladies of the twentieth century. It is strongly linked to many diseases such as heart disease and cancer. Stress is the psychological and physical responses to the demands made of us—the wear and tear of life. Feeling stressed is dangerous when it is prolonged, is experienced too often, or is concentrated on one particular organ of the body.

Adolescents of today experience more stress than did their counterparts in the past. During the last twenty years, stress-related health problems among children and adolescents such as ulcers, high blood pressure, and high cholesterol, have increased dramatically. At the same time, increased family instability, the declining sense of community, the declining role of religion, and the growing impersonalization of the junior high and high school environments mean that adolescents have less support in dealing with stress.

The stress that we feel is seldom from one event but is rather a pile-up of demands from different sources. Based upon national research, the following are the ten major problems and sources of stress which adolescents report experiencing:

Drugs and alcohol
Peer pressure
Family problems
Premarital sex
Lack of concern and attention
Pressure to perform well at school
Financial problems
Pressure to make decisions which they are not ready to make
Concern about friends' and/or parents' drug or alcohol use
Feeling of being alone

A prominent quality of the four thousand high-wellness adolescents in the National Adolescent Wellness Research Project is that they deal effectively with stress. They experience the same stresses as other teens, but they are able to take steps to cope successfully and prevent the level of stress from becoming overwhelming. For this reason they report a lower level of stress than do adolescents who have a lesser degree of personal wellness.

The successful adolescents have shared strategies which have helped them to deal effectively with stress. The strategies work. Furthermore, they can be used by anyone.

Reducing the Load

Randall, a teen from Iowa, had a zest for life and was interested in many different things. He played on the school soccer team, which meant practice every day after school. After that he would deliver his daily paper route. In Boy Scouts he had almost earned his Eagle. His painting was getting better, especially since he had started taking weekly art lessons. At night he took karate lessons three times a week. He met with the chess club once a week, plus tournaments.

Randall was involved. Randall had also become very irritable. He always felt fatigued. He had become noticeably less optimistic. His sense of humor had largely disappeared. Randall was stressed out!

"I had gotten to the point where I wasn't enjoying anything very much," said Randall. "Everything I was involved in was good and interesting. But all together, it was just too much. I had to let some things go. The best thing I could do was to reduce the load. So I made a list of those activities that were the most important to me. I decided to give up the paper route, the Boy Scouts, and karate. I was shocked at the difference this made," he said. "I felt like a great weight had been lifted from my shoulders. I became much less irritable and my sense of humor returned. Life was fun again."

Phil, a teen from Washington, shared that the most helpful strategy he had discovered for dealing with stress was also to reduce the load when life began to feel too stressful. "I really practice this principle," he said. "And try not to let myself get overextended in the first place."

The importance of this principle was impressed upon Phil by the experience of a high school friend. "My friend had everything going for him," said Phil. "He was in several clubs and on the student council. Studying hard had earned him a serious shot at valedictorian. It was especially hard to study now that he was the starting tight end on the football team. When he found extra time he would go volunteer at the local recycling group."

Phil's friend did seem to have everything going for him. The trouble was he apparently had too many things going for him.

"Then right in the middle of his senior year, my friend had a nervous breakdown," said Phil. "I mean he just collapsed. It was not only his emotions and nerves. He was physically exhausted too. It took him six months to recover. The doctors said that he was just doing too much. All of those demands took their toll.

"I will never forget what happened to my friend," said Phil. "I decided that I never wanted to get overextended like that. And I promised myself that I would always be quick to reduce my load of involvements when they began to be too much."

Randall and Phil illustrate a strategy of successfully dealing with stress that is typical of the adolescents with a high degree of wellness. They are good at reducing the load when it gets to be overwhelming. This is difficult to do in our society because we are constantly encouraged to take on more. We are very activity oriented. A cultural belief that is deeply imbedded in our society is "the more activities you are involved in, the better a person you are." This belief, plus modern technology which gives us the opportunity to do more work at a faster pace, prompts us to overextend ourselves and become more susceptible to a high level of stress.

Reducing the load is an effective method of dealing with stress. Its importance is enhanced by the fact that often the *only* way that stress can be decreased and managed in a reasonable way is by reducing the load.

Laughter and a Sense of Humor

Barbara, from Rhode Island, was in a state of shock and disbelief when she was diagnosed with cancer. Everyone in her family was stunned. She was only fifteen years old and she had been in perfect health until recently.

The prognosis was not good. She grew weaker and had to

spend more and more time in bed. The family obtained second and third medical opinions and provided her with the best medical care available. Her family and friends were very supportive of her. Even though everyone did all they could, her condition worsened.

"Many prayers were given on my behalf," said Barbara. "Many people asked about me and I was touched by the great love of those around me.

"One day, someone gave my family a book. The title is *Anatomy of an Illness,* by Norman Cousins.[1] We all read it. The book is about a man, Norman Cousins, who was diagnosed as having a terminal illness. His reactions were much like mine. He also got other medical opinions. They were all the same. The illness was diagnosed as terminal and he was not given very long to live.

"The book describes two actions he took as a last resort to try to heal himself. He persuaded his physician to put him on a megavitamin therapy. The second thing he did really fascinated me and everyone else in my family. He put himself on laughter therapy. He did this because he knew of medical evidence that when we laugh, chemicals are released in our bodies that are healing.

"So we decided to do the same things that Norman Cousins did. We convinced my physician to put me on a megavitamin therapy. Then my family and I developed a laughter therapy program for me. We bought and rented videos that were hilarious to me. I watched them for hours every day. I read jokes. I listened to tapes of comedians. My family and friends told me funny stories. We all laughed a lot."

One year later, the doctors could find no evidence of cancer in Barbara. Her strength and energy had returned. The doctors were surprised.

"I don't know for sure what was responsible for the healing," said Barbara. "But I do feel that the laughter therapy definitely made a difference. I began to feel noticeably better shortly after beginning the laughter therapy. It helped me to develop a greater sense of humor. I began to see more funny things in daily life."

Barbara felt that laughter and humor were important in helping her deal with a very stressful, life-threatening cancer condition. A sense of humor was commonly used by the teenagers in the wellness research project as an effective tool in dealing with stress. Humor helps them in a number of ways.

"Keeping a sense of fun helps me not to take myself too seriously," said Landon, a teen from Nevada. "It's good to be able to laugh at myself sometimes."

"Laughing is a great tension reliever for me," said Stephanie, an adolescent from New Mexico. "Whenever I find myself in a frustrating situation, I try to find something silly in the situation or I will deliberately think about something else that is funny. It helps me to keep from getting so angry or hostile."

"Joking is a way that I can have fun," said a teen from Delaware. "It makes me feel good. My friends and I have a good time when we kid around."

"Seeing the funny side of things helps me to keep a more positive outlook on life," said an adolescent from Missouri. "When I laugh I feel better and problems don't bother me as much."

The teens who have a high degree of wellness use humor as a major coping strategy in dealing with stress. They laugh often and tend not to take themselves too seriously. They seldom use put-downs and sarcasm or engage in jokes at someone else's expense, however. Their brand of teasing is not hostile or hurtful.

Getting Rhythm

Rebecca was stressed out. She felt that if one more demand was made of her she would fall apart. She even found herself resenting the time that was used up when her friends called her on the telephone. She had lost a great deal of her former enthusiasm and was short tempered much of the time.

"I knew something was wrong and that I had to make some kind of change," said Rebecca. "My nerves were on edge and I was out of touch with myself and everyone else.

"One weekend I decided not to do anything or see anyone. I just wanted to be by myself, to be quiet, and to think. I made a list of all the things I had been doing: hours every day with my schoolwork, a part-time job, two school organizations, the school band. My life was full of deadlines and projects to do, and it seemed as if I was always in a hurry and rushing from one activity to another.

"Then it hit me," she said. "There was nothing that I did that was truly recreational. I had no breaks in my life. So I decided I had to change my lifestyle and start doing some things that were relaxing and fun. It began with reading some books that I was interested in . . . just for fun and entertainment. Then I started to play tennis, my favorite sport, about three times a week. I also took up walking every evening. Walking is very relaxing to me.

"Shortly after I started doing these things I felt much better," she said. "I was more relaxed. I enjoyed my daily responsibilities more, and I regained the enthusiasm that I had lost."

Rebecca learned the importance of maintaining periodic breaks of refreshment and recreation in her life. It is a practice which can reduce and prevent stress.

The importance of this practice was illustrated in the book, *Gift from the Sea,* by Ann Lindbergh.[2] The author shares a difficult time in her life when she felt she was becoming emotionally disturbed. Her life was very fast paced and busy and had led her to the point of exhaustion.

Finally, in an act of self-protection, she temporarily withdrew from her hectic life style and retreated to the beach for several days. She went there alone and after a couple of days had passed much of the tenseness left her. It was then that she became aware of the life around her. She walked the beach, collected shells, and watched the tide come in and go out. Everyday, with an unfailing rhythm, the tides came in and returned to the sea. A flash of insight came to her: There is a rhythm to life.

She was struck with the thought that her major problem was that there was not rhythm in her life. Her life had become a nonstop series of deadlines, appointments, projects, and hurried behavior. There had been no breaks, no fun-filled, relaxing pauses.

Restoring rhythm to her life was necessary for her happiness and health. She eventually recovered her rhythm and emotional health by incorporating frequent creative pauses of relaxing and refreshing activities. She believes it is necessary for everyone to do this.

Creative pauses may be taking a walk around the neighborhood, playing golf, playing a game of cards, watching a favorite television program, going to the beach, or hiking in the woods. It can be anything that relaxes, refreshes, and re-creates us.

Frequent creative pauses are important because they add rhythm to our lives. They allow us to break long stretches of physical inactivity with movement. They take us outside for fresh air and sunshine. They allow us to set aside mental challenges (or to interrupt tedium with a mystery or wonder). The adolescents with a high degree of wellness are good at maintaining rhythm in their day-to-day experiences. Many of the participants in our study mentioned a specific activity or hobby that was particularly relaxing or rewarding to them.

"I love photography," said a teen from Oregon. "I like the challenge of taking beautiful pictures."

"I listen to music to relax," said a fourteen-year-old from Michigan. "It makes me feel mellow."

"I enjoy getting in the car and riding around with a couple of friends."

"I play golf a couple of times a week," said an Oklahoma adolescent. "It's fun. It relaxes me. And I love being outdoors."

Enjoy the Process

The father spent most of the lunch hour bragging about his sixteen-year-old son's accomplishments. However, his boasting was mixed with an obvious sense of anxiety and stress. He proudly mentioned more than once that his son had achieved a perfect 4.0 grade point average in high school.

The father emphasized his hope that his son would continue his perfect grades but expressed his fear that he might not succeed. He discussed with intensity the scenario that if his son could maintain a perfect grade point average through high school graduation, he would almost certainly be admitted to a prestigious private university on the West Coast and would probably receive a scholarship as well. He revealed that it had been his dream to attend this university but it had not worked out. Now that his son had a chance, he certainly did not want him to blow it. He longed for his son to accomplish what he had not been able to do. The father's anxiety and stress became obvious when he discussed the feared scenario: His son's grade point would slip and he would have no chance of being admitted to this prestigious university.

What a burden this son carries on his shoulders. He is trying to fulfill the dream of his father to attend a particular university and he consistently receives the message that no other university is really acceptable. Daily he faces intense pressure to maintain perfect grades so that he can make his father's dream come true.

Is it any wonder that the son has high blood pressure problems or that he regularly visits a counseling clinic? It is tragic that learning for him is neither fun nor adventure. Education for him is unpleasant and limited because it is focused entirely on an end product—achieving a perfect grade point average, scoring high on standardized tests, and being accepted into a particular prestigious university. He has missed out on the experience of learning for the joy of it. He has not known the excitement of spontaneous learning, of finding the answers to questions "just because" he wants to know.

A great many adolescents experience intense stress because they place all of their efforts and thoughts on achieving an end product and they ignore the *process* of accomplishing those products. In many ways our society has contributed to the stress among adolescents by encouraging a preoccupation with results quickly achieved.

In our schools, for example, some principals and teachers tend to emphasize an end product, standardized test scores, so much that they teach the children almost exclusively within the confines of doing well on the standardized tests. This happens in part because administrators are under pressure to produce "better products," which translates into higher standardized test scores.

David Elkind, author of *The Hurried Child*[3], states that one consequence of "teaching to the tests" is that standardized tests are now determining school curriculum. As a consequence, our schools are seriously restricting the scope of education. The success of schools is being measured not by the kinds of human beings they produce, but by increases in standardized test scores.

Furthermore, Elkind notes, there is a tendency for school to be viewed as an assembly line in which the objective is to increase production. So a pattern emerges of trying to put in as much in kindergarten as was formerly done in first grade. Why not teach fourth grade math in second grade? The pressure to teach more at earlier grades has resulted in increased stress among children and teachers.

The successful adolescents in the wellness research project are noticeably not fixated on the end products. They enjoy and value the process which leads to an end result. They focus on the journey and not just on reaching the final destination.

Karlos, a New York teen, had played the violin for most of his life. He had taken violin lessons since he was five years old, was talented, and played well. However, his performances at recitals and concerts were disappointing.

"I was miserable at concerts or recitals," he said. "I wanted so much for my performance to be perfect that I tensed up and did not perform well.

"One night I was watching an interview with Ray Charles. In the interview he was asked what he thought was the reason for his musical success. His answer was that he loved making the harmony of the music. He said that he enjoyed putting it together, the creation of the sounds. He enjoyed the practice. He said that he did not play it for the hit records. The hits were nice but he emphasized that he would enjoy playing even if he never had any hit records. Something else Ray Charles said that really impressed me was that he had never heard a great musician who did not thoroughly enjoy what he was doing.

"I realized then," said Karlos, "that I had been concentrating too much on what other people thought of my performance. I had not allowed myself to enjoy the playing for itself."

Karlos changed his approach to the violin. "I disciplined myself to enjoy the process of playing the violin whether it was practice, a concert, or a recital," he said. "I conditioned myself not to be so concerned about what other people thought of my performance. I played back in my mind what Ray Charles had said, and I said to myself every day that if I enjoyed playing and what I was doing, the performance would take care of itself. In a short time I had more pleasure in playing the violin than I ever had. I felt much less stress and tenseness. My recital and concert performances improved so much that it truly surprised my teacher.

"Now I have applied this same philosophy of enjoying the process to other parts of my life," said Karlos. "It works! It has eliminated a lot of stress for me."

Setting Priorities

Frances, an adolescent in New Hampshire, reveals a concern common among teenagers. It is a stress so powerful that it has led many into destructive behavior such as drug abuse, crime, or deliberately hurting others.

"I wanted desperately for other kids to like me," said Frances. "I wanted approval and acceptance and to be popular. Being so self-conscious made me afraid I would say or do the wrong thing or not dress right. I was always trying to act a 'certain' way to be accepted. I was not being myself.

"One night I was talking with my mother about some kids who didn't seem to like me as much as I wanted them to like me," Frances shared. "My mother said something to me that really made an impression.

"She said, 'Sometimes people can like you for the wrong reasons. If they like you because you are acting like someone else, then that is the wrong reason and the friendships won't be real. You're placing too much importance on other people liking you and being popular. That is not the important thing you should be emphasizing. What you should give your attention to is being a friend to others. Concentrate on showing an interest in other people . . . being a good listener . . . being considerate of other people's feelings . . . and helping people when you can. When you do those things, you will have real friends and popularity will take care of itself.'

"I knew that what she was saying was true," said Frances. "I had been trying so hard to be liked and accepted that I wasn't really thinking about *being* a friend. It wasn't easy at first, but I began to tell myself that it didn't matter whether I was popular or not. Instead, I concentrated on *being* a friend to others. I became a better listener, and I learned how to ask questions about someone else's interests and to carry on a conversation with them. I tried to show genuine concern for others. I made an effort to be more thoughtful and considerate. I tried to make other people feel at ease at social occasions. This new way of life gave me more confidence because I had the power to help others. The other way I had no power at all because I was just trying to get other people to like me and hoping I would get their approval. I was totally depending on their reactions to me.

"Things changed for me," said Frances. "Gradually, I felt more comfortable and more real. Good friendships formed for me."

The high-wellness adolescents were skilled at maintaining a clear view of what is truly most important in life. It is a quality which helps them to manage stress effectively.

For example, a Missouri teen said, "I like to set priorities whenever I have to make decisions. It makes it easier to decide and I don't get tensed up."

Brandon, a Pennsylvania teen shared, "In my junior year of high school, I had an opportunity to work with one of the law firms in town. This was great because I knew I wanted to go to law school. I was working there fifteen hours a week."

All went well for a few months. Then Brandon felt the impact of problems arising. "I didn't have the energy to do my homework well and my grades were slipping," he said. "It was a grind going to baseball practice. I was too tired to enjoy it and I wasn't playing well.

"My friends felt slighted because I did not have much time to spend with them. I was also spending less time with my family and my girl friend. I had completely stopped my hobby of fishing, which I enjoyed and found relaxing. In fact, I had very little time to do anything fun."

As the stress mounted, Brandon's health began to suffer. He didn't feel as if he was doing anything well. Finally, a series of unfortunate events got his attention. Brandon worked a little overtime on a rush job at the law firm, was late for a study session with some friends for a test the next day, and completely forgot his girl friend's birthday party.

"I felt like I was constantly running. I was tired of it," said Brandon. "So I stopped, took some time out, and I asked myself what was most important to me. Obviously I could not do everything I was trying to do.

"What was most important were my friends, my girl friend, my family, my health, and my schoolwork. The job with the law firm was nice but not necessary. So I let the job go. I also decided to drop baseball because the job and baseball together took up at least twenty-five hours a week."

Physical Exercise

A common way that the successful teens deal with stress is through exercise. In addition to maintaining a physically active lifestyle they deliberately use exercise as a strategy for reducing tension and stress.

"I like to play tennis three or four times a week," said one teen. "It makes me feel good and it gets rid of a lot of tension."

"When I get upset about something," said Bob from Kansas, "I get my boxing gloves on and hit the punching bag for several minutes. It does wonders."

"I jog just about every day," said a Wisconsin adolescent. "After I start to run, I can feel the stress and the worries just fading away."

"I work out with weights regularly," said a teen from Tennessee. "If I am worried or irritated about something or just feeling particularly stressed out, I will go lift weights as soon as I can. Afterward, my optimism and sense of humor seem to return. My disposition certainly improves."

"Swimming is one of the most relaxing activities in the world to me," said a California youth. "When I swim it feels like every muscle in my body gets a workout. The stressed-out feelings seem to be washed away—no pun intended!"

The adolescents who have a high degree of wellness utilize one of the most effective strategies for coping with stress. Physical exercise increases the blood circulation. Thus oxygen supply to the brain is also increased and helps us to feel more optimistic and confident about life. Tension is substantially reduced with exercise.

An Inner Peace

Every night millions require sleeping tablets in order to sleep. Hypertension and hyperactivity are common maladies of the American culture. Few of us avoid getting caught up in the rush of the day and night. We have become a nation of high-

strung and nervous people with too many of us, at all ages, in a
state of constant agitation.

One quality which the adolescents in our study had somehow developed is the presence of an inner peace. It is really an
attitude of serenity. And this attitude of peace is of great importance in helping them deal with stress successfully.

What gives them this serenity and peace of mind? It is in
part due to the other resources they possess such as good problem-solving ability and a high level of optimism, strong family
relationships, and spiritual faith. But many reported cultivating specific practices to achieve a sense of inward peace.

"Every morning after breakfast I go into a room for a period
of prayer," shares a Minnesota teen. "I ask God to fill me with
strength, wisdom, and energy for the day. Other family members often join me. One of us will read aloud an inspirational
thought from the Bible, from another book, or from a poem.
This takes about fifteen minutes. I feel more peaceful and confident the rest of the day because of those fifteen minutes."

A teen from Louisiana shares the technique of slowing down
enough to observe nature every day. "I try to spend some time
each day just watching nature work," he said. "I will watch the
birds and listen to their songs. They never seem to get in a big
hurry. That makes me feel tranquil inside. Or sometimes I just
sit in the sun and let the rays warm my body. There is a peace
to that. . . ."

Shawn, from Georgia, is an outstanding baseball player who
also excels in academics. Yet he never seems to be in a rush and
has a very relaxed manner. "I deliberately practice an 'easy-
does-it' attitude. I like to do everything without hecticness and
pressure," he said. "It gives me a greater feeling of peace.

"I learned that the best way to hit a baseball is by the easy
method," he said. "That way my muscles are relaxed and coordinated. If I overpress I get tense and don't hit the ball as well.
I try to apply this easy-does-it method to everything I do."

A teen from Oklahoma shared that she likes to visualize peaceful scenes regularly. "Particularly when I am feeling agitated I will visualize the moon sailing high in the heavens or the break of the ocean waves onto the seashore."

Many of the adolescents shared that they internalize certain life philosophies, proverbs or passages from the Bible which help them to maintain a peaceful countenance. The following are just a few examples.

"If God is for me who can be against me." *Romans 8:31*

"The Lord is my light and my salvation; whom shall I fear? The Lord is the strength of my life; of whom shall I be afraid?" *Psalm 27:1*

"There is a silver lining in every cloud."

"This too shall pass."

"What is the worst thing that can happen in this situation I am concerned about and what good can come from it?"

"Take one day at a time."

"Facts can be changed by attitudes."

"If there be a remedy, find it. If there be none, never mind it."

Ways to Help Your Teen Succeed

1. **As a parent, set the example not only in what you say, but in what you do.** Look over your own schedule. Are you overextended at work, at church, or with other organizations? If you find that you really have been doing too much, sit down and prioritize your daily and weekly activities. Choose those that are truly important and get rid of the rest. You will find that you feel better and that you will have more time for yourself and for your family. Be sure that you let your child in on

what you are doing. Talk about what being overextended can do to your life overall.

2. Try to find something to laugh about every day. This could be something funny that you heard someone say, or something you saw on television or at a movie. It could also be something funny that you read somewhere. Most importantly, don't forget to laugh when you do something silly or out of the ordinary. Everyone does something silly every once in a while. It could be that you mispronounced a word, or you mixed up the order of words in a sentence, or that you put the toilet paper in the refrigerator by mistake. Don't take yourself too seriously, and let your teen see your funny bone.

3. Do you have time to sit and be quiet? Do you have times that are devoted solely to activities that are fun and relaxing? After you have made your life less hectic, set aside time to do those things that relax and refresh. Think about things that you enjoy. Do you like to read books, paint, or do crafts? You will need to be deliberate in setting aside time. Encourage your teen and family to do the same.

4. Enjoy the process. Have you ever heard anyone say, "Getting there is half the fun!"? Of course they mean that what happens at the end isn't any more important than getting to the end. Our lives are filled more with processes than with ends. Life itself is a process from birth to the end, death. How do you look at the processes in your life? When you want to get from point A to point B, do you have your eyes on point B most of the time, or are you noticing the trip between A and B? Learn to enjoy the trip. When your teen is working toward a particular goal, praise him or her for the progress made so far and tell how proud you are of the work already accomplished.

Part of this encouragement should also be that regardless of the outcome, you will still love him or her and that you will still be proud.

5. Set aside time to exercise. This may be hard if you are not already in the habit, so be deliberate. Think about activities that you enjoy, such as bike riding, swimming, or jogging. Even walking around the block a few times after dinner will work to relieve stress. When you are physically active you will find that your appetite is better, you will sleep better, and your mind will be alert. Invite other members of your family to join in. Walking together is a great way to spend time together talking and enjoying each other's company, as well as becoming physically fit.

6. Maintain your inner peace and serenity. Do you have inner peace that steadies you through your days? Prayer and meditation are used by many to find inner peace and strength. Do you pray and meditate regularly? Is there a routine that you follow? Let your children in on what you do to keep peace within. Let them take part in what you do and talk with them about how keeping an inner peace helps focus you and strengthens you.

Tips for Teens Who Want to Succeed

1. Understand that there are many opportunities presenting themselves to you right now. There is no way you can choose them all. You want to be in the band, chorus, the school play, and be on the JV volleyball team and somehow keep your grades up. Plus, you still want to have time to hang out with your friends and be involved at church. Sit down and make a list of the activities that are the most important to you. Choose to be involved in just those that are most important and get rid of the rest.

2. Don't take life too seriously. Find something to laugh at everyday. Make sure the humor that you find is the kind that isn't aimed at someone or a group in a negative way. Watch a funny show every once in a while. Read a book of funny stories. Take time to laugh. When you do something silly, don't forget to laugh. You might accidentally wear two different colored socks to school one day, or wear your shirt backward. These are funny things. Don't be afraid to laugh at yourself.

3. Take time to be quiet. Notice things around you in nature or the special people who live with you at home. Do you have a hobby such as photography, drawing, or reading historical novels? Take time to do your hobby. This will be relaxing and help remove stress from your life.

4. Learn to enjoy the work that you do and not just finishing the work. Learn to enjoy getting ready to write the research paper as well as finishing the research paper. Life is a process, so learn to enjoy what you are doing and don't be in such a hurry just to get done. Remember that getting there is half the fun!

5. Lighten the load. Sometimes we take on too much in our daily lives and we want to do everything at once. We want to have lots of friends, we want to improve our personalities, and so on. Oftentimes we find that we place too much importance on things that don't really matter. Sit down and really think about what you view as important and decide if this is something really worth working toward. Decide what is more important and work on that first.

6. Are you physically active? Do you spend a lot of time watching TV or playing video games? Being active can help you to feel better. You will find that you have more energy, you are more alert, and that you can eat that extra slice of pizza without worrying so much about your weight. Think about the kinds of activities you like to do. Do you like swimming, mountain biking, or weight lifting? Even walking casually around the neighborhood after dinner will help you out physically and reduce stress. Decide what you like to do and then do it regularly. Find a friend to ride bikes, walk, or dance with you.

7. Develop an inner peace or serenity that steadies you through your day. If you have it, think about how you make it grow and flourish. If you don't have inner peace, find a trusted adult who you feel has that inner peace and ask him or her how they got it and how he or she keeps it going. Many people find their inner peace through prayer or meditation and reading the Bible or other inspirational books. Make your inner peace a source of strength for yourself.

How Can I . . . ?

1. One way to manage some stresses is to analyze what they are and how you usually react. Then you can consider other, more effective ways of managing the stresses. In the space below, list the two or three circumstances that cause you the most stress. In the next column, describe your typical reaction. In the last column list some possibilities of managing the situation better.

E X A M P L E

What causes me stress?	My typical reaction:	A better way:
demands on time (job, housework, yard, errands, cooking, tests at school)	work longer hours, feel overwhelmed, cramming session, stay up too late, upset stomach	—hire help with house or yard —adjust standards (not perfectly clean is okay) —simpler meals (soup, salad) —review notes and text daily —study with a friend

2. What makes you laugh or cheers you up?

E X A M P L E

Ann, who always has a joke (sometimes naughty)
A Shot in the Dark *(Peter Sellers as Inspector Clouseau)*

3. What is a hobby that refreshes and pleases you? When will you budget time for that hobby?

E X A M P L E

Ceramics—Sunday afternoons
Canoeing—Saturdays; any summer days

FIVE

There Is a Pony in Here
Somewhere: Optimism

· ·

Aproverb passed from generation to generation, particularly among those whose roots reach back to the early years of the shipping industry, suggests the importance of attitude.

> One ship sails East
> Another West
> By the selfsame winds that blow.
> Tis the set of the sails
> And not the gales
> That determine the way they go.

So it is that the quality of our lives is determined not so much by events but by how we look at things, by our attitudes.

There is an old story about a man who lived in rural Arkansas in the middle 1800s. Down on his luck and discouraged, he had lost his job and had no money. His misery was so great that he gave up all hope and said that he just wanted to die. Laziness was a prominent characteristic of this gentleman, which in large part had led to his condition.

So intent was he on pursuing the option of dying that he planned his own funeral. He even persuaded some of his friends to plan a funeral procession. He stopped eating and grew weaker.

As the day of the funeral procession arrived, the gentleman, weak but still alive, decided he might as well witness his own funeral. So he insisted on lying in the casket as the procession began. This really disturbed people in the community. As the procession went down the street there were sounds of weeping and whispering about how terrible this was. One by one, the leading citizens rushed up to the casket and offered to give him various jobs. But with each job offer there was no answer from the casket. One neighbor came to the casket and offered to give the man a piece of land to farm. There was only silence from the casket. The onlookers speculated that he indeed had died.

As the funeral procession neared the cemetery, a farmer with a wagon full of corn and potatoes stopped beside the casket and offered to give him all the corn and potatoes. Some movement could be heard inside the casket. The crowd gasped as the man slowly sat upright. He looked at the farmer a moment and asked, "Is the corn shucked and the potatoes peeled?" The farmer answered, "No, the corn is not shucked and the potatoes are not peeled."

The man shook his head sadly and motioned his hand forward to the driver of the casket. "Drive on," said the man as he slowly reclined his body back down into the casket.

Many of us are more akin to this man than we like to admit. We ignore the resources and opportunities all around us. We don't see the assets and advantages that are present in our lives. Instead, we often focus on problems, what we don't like, or what we don't have. So we find ourselves demonstrating negative attitudes or pessimism.

A very clear and prominent characteristic of the high-wellness adolescents is that they have set the sails of their ships to carry them in a positive direction. They are masters of optimism.

There Is a Pony in Here Somewhere

A story is told of a young boy whose family purchased a home in the country. The boy brought a friend to visit their new home and after running over the grounds for a while, they visited the barn in the back.

The barn had not been cleaned out in some time by the previous owners. The highly aromatic evidence of an abundance of manure greeted the boys as soon as they went into the barn. The friend screamed, "Oh yuk! This smells disgusting. Don't you smell it?"

"Yes, I smell it," answered the boy as he looked with anticipation through the barn. "But it doesn't bother me."

The boy's friend replied, "Well I can't stand it. Let's leave. Why are you staying in here?" With great excitement the boy said, "Because I know that with all this manure there has to be a pony in here somewhere!"

In this young boy we see the essence of an optimist. An optimist takes an unattractive or negative situation and sees something good in it.

The successful adolescents in the wellness study have a high degree of optimism. They look on the bright side of things. The ability to find something good in a bad situation is a common characteristic of these teens. They possess a deep and undaunted belief that everything will turn out for the best. This belief is strongly reinforced by their spiritual faith and by the conviction that the force for good is dominant in life.

Brian was considered one of the most outstanding high school quarterbacks in the state of Georgia. A number of universities recruited him. He finally decided to go to the University of Alabama. He spent his first three years playing behind another young man who was enjoying phenomenal success as Alabama's starting quarterback. When the starting quarterback was seriously injured during the season, Brian expected that he would step up to quarterback the Crimson Tide of Alabama.

Brian was stunned with disappointment when he was bypassed. Instead, the starting quarterback job was assigned to the team's outstanding wide receiver. Because he possessed great quickness and speed, the coaches felt that he could make things happen offensively by playing at that position. And he had played at quarterback in high school.

Brian struggled with the natural feeling of being rejected. He was certain that the coaches lacked confidence in him. A mood of depression surfaced. But Brian did not allow those negative feelings, as logical as they were, to have dominance over his thought pattern. He began consciously to affirm the good things in his situation: good friends, support from his teammates, outstanding coaches, and his own talent.

He also did something else which was important to him. He looked upon this situation as an opportunity. Brian, in his own way, was "finding a pony in the barn."

"I think what helped me to get over the discouragement was reminding myself that my purpose in life extends far beyond myself and my goals," said Brian. "My purpose is much greater than whether I become the starting quarterback. That's really pretty limited.

"My purpose in life is to help other people," said Brian. "Everybody goes through discouragement and disappointments. A lot of people have a really hard time dealing with them.

"So I decided that this was a great opportunity for me to help other people learn to deal with their disappointments better. If I did not let this situation get me down, if I could keep my attitude and actions constructive, I could help others through my example."

Brian succeeded. His attitude and actions were very positive during this trying time. Even though some sports columnists were communicating the expectation that he would feel resentment, Brian's lack of resentment and discouragement were very apparent to those around him.

Toward the end of that season a change of circumstances resulted in Brian being selected as the starting quarterback. He responded by guiding Alabama to a Gator Bowl victory over North Carolina. Brian played superbly and was named the "Most Valuable Player" of the Gator Bowl.

Through his ability to see an opportunity in a discouraging set of circumstances, Brian turned a negative situation into a positive one. He helped others and himself by taking advantage of an opportunity to fulfill a purpose that was larger than his self-centered goals.

John S., a teen from Wisconsin, had a dream of going to college. He knew exactly what he wanted to do. His goal was to get a degree in Mechanical Engineering. He planned ahead and submitted several applications for scholarships. John's mother had always encouraged him in his schoolwork and she strongly supported his ambition to attend college.

His dreams were dashed when he received replies to his scholarship applications, one by one, turning him down. As the head of a single-parent family, John's mother had always managed to provide John and his younger sisters with what they needed. But now she could not give John what he needed and what she desperately wanted to give him—a college education! Money had always been tight and there was just no way she could afford to send John to college. The family's debts were great and their income was limited to the extent that they could not qualify for a loan to pay for tuition.

"I felt pretty low about it," said John. "My dream had been snatched away from me. The future did not look promising.

"Finally, I decided I had to snap out of it and do the best I could with the opportunities available. I looked around and found a job as a mechanic. The pay was decent and the fellow who owned the shop had been a friend of the family for years. I had always been good with cars and I enjoyed working on them. I soon learned how to do body work and I began to do more and more of that type of work."

About a year later, John's mother became ill and was unable to work. He became the sole supporter of the family. It was hard to make ends meet but he managed. John was good at his work and increasingly people brought him their cars for repairs and body work. "I gradually came to realize that I was lucky. I was doing something I was good at doing and I enjoyed doing," said John. "Not many people can say that."

Then John looked for and found another pony in his barn. "I was at an antique car show at our mall when it dawned on me that I had everything I needed to restore old cars. So I started my own small business and did all the work by myself in the beginning. It was exciting to me to take junked cars and restore them to their splendor," said John, "and I knew there was a market for them."

John bought old cars that nobody wanted, restored them, and then sold them for a profit. His cars looked and ran good. The word spread rapidly and his business prospered.

Today John is financially secure and provides for all the needs of his mother. He also made it possible for his sisters to have the college education which he did not receive. He looked for something good in a negative situation and he found it.

Breaking the Chains of Fear

Charles Dickens made an insightful observation about the human condition: "We wear the chains we forge in life." We often do forge chains of fear and pessimism until we become bound by them. Interestingly, we can come to embrace our chains of fear as though we love them. We act as though the chains of fear are reality and insist that they cannot be broken. We focus on our concerns and frustrations so much that they consume our thoughts. A pattern of constant worry develops and nagging anxiety is experienced. And a terrible cycle is set: fear → tension/worry → whatever is feared happens → more fear → more tension/worry → and on and on.

We do not have to be enslaved by chains of fear. We can break the chains by changing our thoughts. It has been noted that people are what they think rather than what they say, read, or hear. Persistent, positive thinking can undo any condition.

Ralph, an Ohio teen, was plagued by a fear that had haunted him since childhood. He was afraid people would laugh and make fun of the way he talked. He had a tendency to stutter when he spoke. He was very self-conscious about his speech and when possible, he would avoid being with large groups or with people he did not know and trust.

He was tormented when he was called upon to answer a question or to give an oral report in school. He was terrified that he would stutter. The intense fear he felt made him very anxious and actually increased his tendency to stutter. His fear was bringing into reality what he feared.

"I was paralyzed with dread," said Ralph. "It became un-bearable for me to go to school. One day I was called on to answer a question in my English class. I knew the answer but when I tried to respond I began to stutter. I could not stop stuttering. I felt like a fool. I walked out of the classroom in a rage. I walked away from school that day and made up my mind that I was not going to return. My parents were morti-fied. But I would not listen to their attempts to reason with me. I did not intend to return to school and subject myself to any more humiliation.

"I was surprised the next day when a car pulled into our driveway and my English teacher, Mrs. Turner, got out. She asked if she could talk to me privately. So we went into the living room and sat down.

"Before Mrs. Turner could say anything, I told her I was dropping out of school," Ralph continued. "She told me she did not want me to do that. She said that I had a lot of ability and could be successful at anything I put my mind to. I told her it would be hard for anyone who couldn't talk to be success-ful.

"I remember she looked me straight in the eyes and said, 'Ralph, you don't have to have life be easy in order to be successful. I know you have a fear of talking in public, but dropping out of school won't help. It will only make it worse. You can overcome this problem. The most important thing you can do to conquer this or any fear is to go on the offensive and meet it head on.'"

She gave Ralph a book to read which had a great impact on him. The book contained information about Demosthenes.

Demosthenes was a great Greek orator. In fact, he is consid-ered one of the greatest speakers in history. However, it was not always so. Demosthenes experienced serious problems with his speech. His voice had an unpleasant sound, his lungs were weak, and he spoke in an awkward manner. He overcame great difficulties and trained himself to become one of the greatest orators in history by reciting as he climbed steep hills and by shouting above the roar of ocean waves with his mouth full of pebbles.

"His story was an inspiration to me," said Ralph. "I mean, if Demosthenes was willing to shout above the roar of the ocean with his mouth full of pebbles, then I could make more of an effort.

"The idea of turning my speech problem into an asset was fascinating to me. So with Mrs. Turner's encouragement I decided to go on the offensive to meet the problem head on. I joined the speech club.

"The first few meetings were miserable and there were times when I wanted to quit. But I stayed with it. I actually came to enjoy the speech club and one unexpected development was that I made some friends from this experience. As I learned how to prepare for public speaking, the more I spoke in public, the more comfortable I felt about it. I was surprised when I realized that I was losing my fear and that my stuttering was much less frequent."

Harmony of the Rainbow

Lydia participated on the school gymnastics team. She possesses a great deal of ability and she had learned the proper techniques. But unfortunately when she competed in school meets, a strange phenomena occurred. She did not perform well and usually received disappointing scores. Lydia, of course, became very discouraged about the situation. Her sense of frustration increased as some of her peers began to criticize and ridicule her gymnastics.

One day her coach took her aside and suggested to Lydia that perhaps her problem was that she was dreading the gymnastics meets and the dread or fear was causing her to become tense and not perform well. The coach encouraged her to enjoy the process of her routines and stop worrying about the end result.

"My coach told me that I needed to get more of a sense of harmony in my movements," said Lydia. "She said she wanted me to feel that harmony inside and then perform with harmony. To help me do this she gave me a picture of a rainbow and asked me to look at it every day. She asked me to notice the way the colors blended together and created such a beautiful effect—that's harmony!"

Lydia looked at the rainbow and meditated upon the harmony of the colors before every practice and before each gymnastics meet. This had a surprising effect on her. "I began to visualize myself moving with the same kind of harmony as the colors of the rainbow," she said. "As I relaxed, my movements actually did become more harmonious. I found myself enjoying the process of gymnastics—the movement, the control—much more. I would be so intently focused on my routine and music that I would forget all about the audience or the other gymnasts. My performance improved a lot and I received much better scores in the meets."

There is a rhythm to life—an ebb and flow. When we feel in tune with the rhythm of life around us, we experience connectedness. When we are in touch with our feelings and we have a strong sense of inner harmony, we feel optimistic and that life is good.

An inner harmony was characteristic of the adolescents in the National Adolescent Wellness Research Project. Many had cultivated this sense of inner harmony and joy through such avenues as reading poetry or inspiring biographies, listening to relaxing or rhythmic music, meditating, praying, turning to their spiritual faith, taking walks in the woods, or looking at beautiful works of art.

The sense of inner harmony helps to reduce their level of

stress and frustration. They have the quiet conviction that they can handle life. This sense of harmony certainly reinforces their optimism. Their optimism in turn enhances their inner harmony. And so another kind of cycle is set: harmony/peace → control/success in meeting life's challenges → peace → and on and on.

There Is No Defeat or Failure

Kristian, a graduating senior, received a standing ovation as he completed his address to 1,300 students at Class Day at Grand Island High School in Grand Island, Nebraska. It was an inspirational speech. The students were inspired not just because of the speech, but because they knew Kristian. He was the inspiration.

Kristian spent the summer following graduation the same way he had spent the previous summer—as a YMCA camp counselor. In the fall he entered college. He received two scholarships and has now completed his first year of college with A's and B's. He was particularly pleased with his first year of college because academics had always been hard for him.

In fact, life has been hard for Kristian from the beginning. Kristian was born with no fingers and no feet. Moreover, he was born with crossed eyes, a cleft palate, and neurological problems.

His biological mother decided to give him up for adoption soon after he was born. His life was to be changed dramatically when he was adopted by a loving couple who were themselves physically challenged. His mother, Vernita, is blind, and his father, Bob, had been born without one arm. But his adoptive parents are not handicapped in their love for him and in the time they devoted to him. They also taught him a priceless lesson—to be a tough-minded optimist.

"I learned from my parents that there is no defeat or failure," said Kristian. "Failure only exists if you accept that as your reality. I watched my parents continually be faced with failure, or disappointment while I was growing up. But they refused to respond to the defeat or failure. Instead they kept their eyes on the goal they wanted to achieve. And they were usually successful.

"When I was a child, my cleft palate made it difficult for others to understand my speech," Kristian continued. "I spent many hours working with a speech pathologist who taught me important things in addition to helping me speak more clearly. She taught me to negotiate for myself, to express my wants and needs in a polite way, and to be the best I could be. She helped me to be more patient with myself and not to feel like a failure when I did not speak perfectly. I was taught to recognize the positives in my life and to concentrate more on the progress I was making with my speech rather than on the work I still had to do."

Kristian's refusal to accept defeat and his ability to see the positives in his life have enabled him to accomplish remarkable success. Despite the problems and frustrations he has experienced, he is considered by his friends and teachers as one of the most positive and optimistic adolescents in the state of Nebraska. He is looked to by many as a role model.

"There is no defeat or failure." Kristian's words are powerful. They represent the tough-minded optimism of the successful adolescents in our research project.

Because Things Are Bad Now Doesn't Mean They Will Stay That Way

Sharon was having a bad time. She and her family had moved to another part of the country. It was in the middle of the school year and Sharon was in the tenth grade. She had left friends and familiar places behind. Many difficult adjustments had to be made.

Sharon felt loneliness and isolation as she had never before experienced. She did not seem to fit in at her new school. "The new school was very cliquish and for whatever reason I was not accepted," she said.

Her physical development was not as advanced as some of the other girls, so she was not receiving as much attention from the boys. She was not athletic nor did she play a musical instrument. She just did not seem to fit in with any of the groups at school.

"The only thing I was good at was art. I was making pretty good grades. Some of the girls at school thought I was too intellectual, so they regularly made a point of saying mean things to me. I was miserable—no friends, no dates. I had never felt so alone in my life.

"I talked to my parents about it," said Sharon. "They wanted to help but there was not much they could do except listen. There were no other school options. There was one private school in town, but my parents could not afford the tuition—and it was probably even more cliquish."

One evening, Sharon was in her room crying. Her mother came in and sat down beside her. When she asked her what was wrong, Sharon replied that she felt like "a loser."

"I will never forget our conversation that evening," Sharon said. "My mother told me I was not a loser. She told me that I was a beautiful person and that I would meet a lot of people in life who saw me that way. She said that bad times don't last forever. She encouraged me to hang in there and be patient.

"I pointed out to her that nobody liked me and that I had no friends. My mother then said something that took hold of me. She said, 'Because things are bad now doesn't mean they will stay that way.'"

Sharon's mother gave her some biographies of famous people to read. "It was fascinating to learn that these highly successful people had not always been successful and well-liked," said Sharon. "I was shocked to learn that Winston Churchill did not do well in secondary school and his father didn't even think he was very intelligent. Elvis Presley was not popular in high school. I guess I thought he was always popular and admired by others.

"The thought that my situation would not stay the same forever and that my life would get better was a gift to my mental health. It made me feel much more hopeful. I relaxed a lot. I concentrated on academics and getting better as an artist."

In time, things did change for Sharon. She developed a close friendship with a girl in her art class. Her art began to be exhibited widely in her community and area of the state. From this she received some well-deserved recognition and acclaim. After high school graduation, she went on to college where she excelled academically and enjoyed a full social life.

"Because things are bad now doesn't mean they will stay that way." What an important truth to remember! This thought is the essence of optimism and was an important source of encouragement and hope for the adolescents in our wellness research project. This truth has been illustrated in the lives of many people. The following case histories are examples:

Girl, orphaned, willed to custody of grandmother by mother, who was separated from alcoholic husband, now deceased. Mother rejected homely child. . . . Grandmother resolves to be more strict with granddaughter . . . dresses granddaughter oddly . . . refuses to let her have playmates . . . does not send her to grade school.

Boy, secondary school, has obtained certificate from physician stating that nervous breakdown makes it necessary for him to leave school for six months. Boy not a good all-around student . . . has no friends . . . teachers find him a problem . . . spoke late . . . father ashamed of son's lack of athletic ability . . . poor adjustment to school. Boy has odd mannerisms. . . .[1]

These two case histories are from the biographies of Eleanor Roosevelt and Albert Einstein. They certainly illustrate that people can experience lack of success, lack of friends, and lack of self-esteem-building experiences in an earlier period of life and yet end up quite successful. This is a message that the teens who have a high degree of personal wellness had internalized.

Hope

Hope is one of our most vital emotional needs. Hope is an expectation that something good will be fulfilled in our lives— a conviction that there is promise for the future. Hope helps us to face another day, or to try again, or to forgive someone.

The most deeply disturbing problem of youth today is diminishing hope. A tragic evidence of this is that the suicide rate among adolescents has tripled during the last thirty years, according to the United States Bureau of the Census.

Adolescents today live in a situation in which stressors have increased at the same time that the support for dealing with stressors has decreased. Modern teens, for example, experience more loss of parent and family stability due to divorce which in turn decreases their sense of security.[2] There is more freedom to become sexually active and to become involved in drug abuse at younger ages. America has the highest rate of drug abuse and has become the most violent of advanced nations. Teen pregnancies are epidemic and 45 percent of them end in abortion.

Today's teens are the first generation that apparently will not exceed the accomplishments of their parents. They feel threatened by the specter of a "have" and "have not" society. A sense of hopelessness is generated by the growing awareness that a college degree is no longer necessarily a ticket to success.

These are just some of the conditions in our society which have caused many adolescents to lose their belief that the world is a good place in which to live, work, and have a family. These conditions of our society also constitute good reasons why it is important for youth purposely to cultivate a sense of hope. Without hope, we despair. Our behavior is completely different when we are in possession of hope.

Yolanda lay in her own blood on the side of the empty Los Angeles street. She looked up at the streetlights which were quickly growing dim. As the light completely disappeared, she could hear the sound of sirens coming closer.

The doctors and nurses worked intensely to stop the bleeding. The knife wounds were multiple and they were deep. Yolanda almost died that night, but somehow she made it through. The crises point passed in a few days. She was going to live.

Over the next days, Yolanda lay in her hospital bed thinking about her life, which had almost ended in the brutal gang fight. She had thought she might die young. But to come this near to death felt different than she expected. Perhaps she did not really believe it could happen to her. After all, she had always been the one who had prevailed before. She was widely feared on the streets as a fighter and a gang leader.

One afternoon as she was waking from a deep sleep she was aware of a man sitting beside her bed. She did not recognize him. He asked her how she was feeling, visited with her briefly, and left. He returned the next day at about the same time. His visits became a regular occurrence. Sometimes they would talk very little if she was tired. But she felt comfortable with him and enjoyed his visits.

The man brought a deck of cards with him on one of his visits. They played several card games and he won every game. After the last game, he said, "I want to show you something. Look closely at the cards. They are marked. You have been playing against a stacked deck. That's why you've been losing. You had no chance to win. That's what you've been doing with your life, too," he told her. "You've been playing against a stacked deck. You're going to have to get a different deck of cards if you want your life to be different." He then stood up and walked out of the room.

She thought a great deal about playing against a stacked deck. "I knew he was right," Yolanda said. "Several of my friends were already dead or in prison or their brains were messed up with drugs. I knew if I continued on the path I was walking I was going to lose, just like my friends."

Even so, Yolanda was not pleased to see the man when he returned in a few days. She was in a state of agitation. She told him she knew she was playing a set of cards that were stacked against her, but those were the cards life had dealt her and that's the only deck she possessed. She insisted there was no hope for anything else. His suggestion that she get another deck of cards was a lot of bunk.

"The man smiled at me and said that we all have the power to choose a different deck of cards. Then he told me the best was yet to be and that ahead of me was an opportunity for a better way of life."

When he left that afternoon, Yolanda never saw the man again. She tried to reach him a number of times but could never find him.

"About a month later, I received a call from my cousin who lived in Georgia. He asked me to come and take care of his mother who was in poor health," said Yolanda. "She had always been one of my favorite aunts. He went on to tell me that he would send me to vocational school and pay for my living expenses."

The more Yolanda thought about it, the more excited she became. She felt deep inside that this was an opportunity for a better life. This was the different deck of cards she could take.

"For the first time I had hope," said Yolanda. "Now there was hope that a better life was possible and that I could become a better person."

Yolanda followed that hope. She accepted her cousin's invitation and started over in Georgia. Her new life was not always easy, but she was a part of a close family unit. She completed vocational school and secured a good paying job in her chosen vocation. She also has been an effective volunteer in working with troubled youth in the community. "This is something I intend to do for as long as I can," she said. "I can help these kids because I have been there. If I can give just one a glimmer of hope and help them see there is a better way of life, then it's all worth the effort."

Finding hope was crucial for Yolanda. Not only did hope help her to turn her life around, it probably saved her life!

The teens who have a high degree of personal wellness are empowered by hope. They have an *expectancy* of good in their lives. They believe in the supremacy of innate goodness in the course of life events. Hope gives them something to hold on to and instills courage and enthusiasm for facing the challenges of life.

Ways to Help Your Teen Succeed

1. What is your general philosophy of life? Do you believe that good will win out over evil? Do you believe that everything will work out in the end and that even the most pitiful of circumstances can have a positive side? Examine your view of everyday life. When you get up in the morning, find something good about the day. Instead of being sad because the rain is keeping you in, be happy that the county drought situation is going to be eased. Work at seeing the glass as half full instead of half empty. Speak in positive terms about life even when events seem hopeless. Be aware of resources that you have even when you feel as though you have nothing. If a door closes, look for the opened window. This may sound trite, but there is always a way.

2. Do you let your fear of something stop you in your tracks? Most of the things that we are afraid of and worry about never happen. However, fear may cause us to be tense and consequently less effective in what we do. Do you control your thoughts or do your thoughts control you? Make an effort to think in ways that are positive and encouraging both about yourself and others. If you are having negative feelings, acknowledge those feelings and then resolve to put those feelings behind you in order to embrace positive feelings. Positive thinking does affect the way we feel and behave; actions and thought do go together.

3. See the rhythm all around! There is rhythm in the rising and setting of the sun, in the changing of the seasons, and in life itself. Don't allow a hurried schedule to make you so tired that you lose your sense of life's rhythm. When we are tired and stressed, we lose a great deal from our lives: our sense of humor, our sense of hope, and our sense of being connected with those around us. Take time out to enjoy a sunset, or to linger over coffee with a special loved one. Life is too good to miss. Show your teen this very fact not by words, but by your example. Include them in some lingering. Don't be in such a hurry to get from one place to another. In ten years it won't matter that you were five minutes late, but your attitude toward life will matter to your teen years from now.

4. To the best of your ability, remove defeat and failure from your vocabulary. It has been noted that neither success nor failure is ever completely final. There can never be defeat or failure if we learn from our mistakes and go on to become better than we were before. How do you handle things when you have worked and labored to accomplish something only to have it come apart? Do you despair, or do you learn from your mistakes? Do you brush yourself off and continue, or do you decide to quit? Think of the runner who falls and becomes injured in a marathon. The runner knows that he (or she) will not even finish with the top ten finalists, but he picks himself up and limps to the finish line. For this runner, there is no failure or defeat. Resolve to have this attitude in your life.

5. Just as we know that winter will turn into spring, we know that bad times don't last forever. Knowing this makes bad times easier to handle. You can stand it a little longer because you know it won't last forever. As adults we need to remind ourselves that this is true. We sometimes forget, and our teens who have not seen these things personally, need reassuring. When your teen is struggling with a difficult time, be available to listen and reassure. Your own struggles and heartaches become proving grounds for your teens. They watch your attitudes and listen for your words. Show them that there is room for optimism because bad times won't go on forever.

6. Keep hope alive in your life. Hope can take many forms: hope of life after death, or hope that life will improve, or hope that you can have a different life than the one you have right now. Whatever form hope takes for you, express this to your child by the way in which you live your life and what you focus your thoughts on.

Tips for Teens Who Want to Succeed

1. Look carefully at your attitudes toward life and the events surrounding your life. Do you have habits or attitudes that hold you back? You might even go to a trusted adult and ask if they see anything in your personality or habits that could be holding you back. Be prepared for truthful answers that might not necessarily be what you want to hear. Prioritize the points you want to work on and then work on them one at a time.

2. Look for the positives in difficult situations. Do you look for resources that would bring you help in tough times? Look at your philosophy of life. Do you believe that things will work out for the best? Work on being positive and optimistic. Train yourself to find something good in every situation.

3. Face your fears. Are you afraid of looking ridiculous in front of others or getting a B− on an exam? Are you afraid of not getting into the college of your choice or of not getting into college at all? Most of the things that we are afraid of or worry about never happen. Learn to control your thoughts and not let your fears stop you in your tracks. Make yourself think in positive ways about your actions. Visualize yourself doing well, being safe and successful.

4. Understand that there is a rhythm and flow to life. If you are stressed out by overscheduling or overindulging in any one thing, your life is out of balance. Focus on the activities that are really important. Simplify your life. Plan for times of quiet and times for activities that will refresh your spirit. Also, be sure to get enough rest and try to eat a variety of good foods.

5. Practice the principle that you can never be defeated. Each time you miss whatever mark was set, you have a chance to learn and become better than you were before. Don't measure who you are only by the great feats that you accomplish, measure yourself by how you overcome your obstacles.

6. Remember that life is always moving and changing. It doesn't stay the same. The way things are now will not be how they are forever. When you are going through a tough time, do you despair and feel hopeless, or do you have confidence that it will eventually be different? Always tell yourself in times of trouble that just because things are bad now, it doesn't mean they will be bad forever.

How Can I . . . ?

1. We all face disappointments in life. Yet we need not allow those setbacks to devastate us. We can often turn a disappointment into a positive force in our lives by redefining the situation. Shift your focus from the "bad" to the "good."

E X A M P L E

A major disap-pointment I have recently faced:	Something good in this situation:	How I can use the good to respond in a positive way:
having to drive an old "clunker" car because new ones are too costly	*insurance is cheaper, less worry about vandalism*	*save money to buy better car or nicer sound system*

2. Sometimes we allow fears or concerns to discourage us and cause unnecessary worry. It is often helpful to ask, "What is the *worst* thing that can happen?" The worst may not be so terribly awful or may be very unlikely to happen.

E X A M P L E

A fear/worry I have:	The worst that could happen:	How I can conquer/ control this fear/ worry:
that I won't have lots of friends	*that I will be all alone*	*remind myself of two good lifelong friends, remember love of family*

3. Make a list of good things, circumstances, blessings in your life. Count your blessings and be thankful.

E X A M P L E

good health
friends
nice home

SIX

Things Unseen: Spiritual Wellness

· ·

Eight-year-old Derrick fought desperately with the two older boys in the vacant apartment on the South Side. He was trying to protect his five-year-old brother. But this wasn't an ordinary fight. In fact, Derrick was fighting for the life of his younger brother.

The two older boys were determined to kill five-year-old Eric. The reason? Because he would not steal candy for them!

The struggle was fierce and ended at the window of the fourteenth-floor apartment. Despite Derrick's brave efforts, the two older boys had maneuvered Eric to the window and were pushing him out.

Derrick pulled his brother back from the edge once. He made a heroic effort to hold on to his brother, but one of the older boys bit his arm and Derrick lost his grip. Eric Morris plunged fourteen floors to his death.[1]

A national talk show featured a panel of persons who are HIV positive discussing how their lives are affected by the disease. They spoke of changed perspectives and lifestyles. When asked how their sexual relationships have changed, most mentioned a responsibility to inform partners of their HIV status. One woman mentioned that she was having sexual relationships with several people. Had she informed her sexual partners that she was HIV positive? No, she had not and had no intentions of doing so. In fact, she stated that she wanted to give the virus responsible for AIDS to as many people as she could.

A group of teens made headlines in newspapers across the nation. Their story was horrifying. They were members of a cult, and they had brutally murdered another boy. They tortured their victim by gouging out his eyes before killing him.

Other newspaper stories told of seventeen-year-old Eric R. who exploded at his parents when they told him he needed to do better in school. He fumed when they refused to buy him a car before he turned eighteen.

His anger turned deadly in a conspiracy with a friend to murder his parents. The two teens plotted for a week. They duct-taped the bottoms of their shoes to disguise their footprints, put tape over the car's license plate, and wore stockings over their heads. Then Eric watched his plan unfold as his friend stabbed his father twenty-two times and his mother twenty-nine times.

Stories like these are incredibly disturbing. They are distressing because of the terrible acts of violence and harm that people do to others. These events also disturb us because they bring to our attention a great void, a lack of caring, an absence of humanity.

These heinous acts reflect a lack of regard for human life—an absence of a sense of right and wrong. They make clear the consequences of a life empty of anything spiritual.

In contrast to the examples of cruelty and the evil mentioned above, the lives of our four thousand high-wellness adolescents portray a genuine caring and respect for human life. They possess a strong spiritual dimension which has a powerful influence on other aspects of their lives. Their spiritual faith is a very personal, practical, day-to-day experience for them. It is not simply a theological, theoretical, or doctrinal issue.

These teenagers commonly shared that their spiritual faith was a great source of help to them in their relationships, in dealing with stress and crises, and in maintaining a positive outlook toward life. Their spiritual faith helped to give them something important that we cannot do without—hope.

Spirituality Brings Healing

Although Angie had lived in Idaho all of her life, the winter of her fourteenth year seemed colder and more desolate than any she had ever known. She felt a coldness and an emptiness inside, for the recent death of her mother had devastated Angie.

Her crying diminished as the months passed, but tears were replaced by bitterness. She wasn't sure what she was resentful about. Perhaps it was anger at her mother for leaving her. Maybe it was frustration at her father and brothers for not filling the great emptiness she felt.

Whatever the source of her discontent, it swelled inside Angie and influenced her relationships with her family and with others. She was continually in conflict with her father and brothers and would fly into rages over trivial issues.

Her wrath and contentious behavior were not confined to

home. She was defiant toward her teachers and lashed out at classmates. She began to run with a crowd that drank alcohol and used drugs. Her grades dropped.

Angie was trying desperately to find something to make her feel better. She wanted her father and brothers to take away her loneliness, but although they seemed connected with each other, she felt as though she were an outsider when she was with them. Neither her new friends, nor alcohol and drugs, could help. Instead Angie sank further into despair.

"One night, I found myself sitting alone in my room contemplating how I might kill myself," said Angie. "I remember screaming, 'I can't go on like this!' I fell to the floor, pounding my fists against it, crying until I was exhausted. Then I knew what I could do. I remembered that in my mother's nightstand were sleeping pills. I could go to sleep and stop hurting." I opened the drawer where she had stored her pills and saw an unfamiliar book." Angie continued, "It was a journal my mother had kept. I was curious, so I started to read."

What Angie read was her mother's account of her physical and emotional struggles with her illness in the months before her death. She had mourned for events she knew she would never see, such as Angie's high school graduation, wedding, and the birth of her grandchildren.

"I began to feel very selfish. I had been consumed with what had happened to me, how much *I* had lost, how badly *I* was being treated. I had lost sight of my mother's pain and loss. In her last entries she wrote of peace and going home to God. She had hopes that we—my father, brothers, and I—would be able to help each other. Her prayer was that she had taught us enough and had given us something that would help us to live well.

"Then I began to pray. I had never prayed this way before. I don't know how to describe it, except maybe to say I prayed with all of my heart and soul. I said, 'God, I don't want to feel this way anymore. I can't get rid of the anger and hurt by myself. Take it away for me and replace it with your spirit of peace.' I can't put into words the feeling I had after that prayer," said Angie. "There was definitely a feeling of warmth and a feeling of being loved. I did not feel so alone any longer."

Circumstances did not change immediately. She continued to experience depression and anger. But slowly the emotions and attitude began to improve. The behavioral problems at school diminished, and the alcohol use stopped. Her relationships became much more pleasant.

"I changed," said Angie. "My attitude was different. I felt at peace with myself. Somehow I came to better terms with my mother's death. I became a much nicer person once that deep anger was gone. I still miss my mother; I still cry for losing her. I came to see that my father and brothers miss her, too. They just didn't know how to help me. Now I ask for a hug or time to be together with them.

"I don't think all of this could have happened without the hand of God," she continued. "I am so thankful for what started to happen when I found my mother's journal. This whole experience has made me decide that I want to go into a career as a Christian family counselor someday. I know there are many people who are hurting just like I was. I think I could help them."

Angie experienced healing. Her spiritual faith helped to heal a deep emotional wound. She did what was typical of many of the successful teens in our study. She tapped into the powerful resource of spiritual faith to heal deep hurts. Over and over again, the teens we studied told us that the spiritual dimension was a powerful force in helping to overcome grief, disappointments, crises, and stress.

Drawing from a Higher Power

Jamail is fifteen years old and has always lived in the inner city of St. Louis. During his life, he has known many wonderful people in his neighborhood. Unfortunately, violence is commonplace here. Although Jamail had managed to avoid getting involved in violence, he recently faced a situation that he could not sidestep.

A young man from the next street had begun taunting him. He was a year or so older than Jamail, muscular, big, loud, and overbearing. He was, in short, the perfect bully. At first, he called Jamail names and yelled obscenities at him whenever they encountered each other on the streets or at school. On two occasions, he demanded that Jamail give him his money; Jamail complied in order to avoid trouble.

Jamail was humiliated but knew he wouldn't stand a chance in a fight with the bully. In fact, he could be killed. He was sick with fear and shame.

Jamail started shadow boxing everyday after school to help relieve his tension. The idea of actually fighting his nemesis was laughable, but his boxing helped him to deal with his situation. Nevertheless, as the weeks passed, the taunting turned more serious. Jamail was horrified when the bully yelled at him, "I'm going to [rape] your little sister." Over the next few days, the older boy repeated his intentions a number of times saying, "Some time soon. You don't know when or where; I'm going to get her."

The talk on the street was that he had raped before. He was a member of a serious gang. Jamail could not let this happen to his thirteen-year-old sister. But what could he do?

He needed to talk with someone. He turned to his grand-mother, because they had always been able to talk about anything. As they sat down at the kitchen table he told her the whole story. After he had finished, his grandmother was silent for a moment. Then she suggested, "We could call the police."

Jamail answered, "Yes, but the police can't go with me and my sister. They can't guard our house 'round the clock."

Grandmother, a rugged warrior of many life battles, looked at him and said, "You're going to have to take care of this, aren't you?"

"Yes," replied Jamail without hesitating. "But I'm afraid."

"Jamail," his grandmother said, "don't you think that David must have felt just like this when he faced Goliath?"

Jamail did not answer.

"What gave David the courage to face Goliath was that he completely trusted God to protect him," his grandmother continued. "David knew that God was the source of his strength, and he thought more about the power of God than he did the power of Goliath."

Jamail had to admit to himself that he had been focused on the power of the bully, not thinking much about the power of God to help him.

"I wish I could take care of this for you, but I can't," she said. "I can't tell you what to do. But what I can tell you for a fact is that God will help you and God is greater than any hoodlum, Jamail. Depend on Him to give you strength."

Neither of them spoke for a moment. Grandmother got up from the table, walked over to the oven, and took out a pan of corn bread that had been baking. She set the corn bread on top of the stove and quietly said, "The Bible promises that God will give angels charge over you to keep you in all your ways." She was referring to Psalm 91:11.

Their conversation ended with a few more assurances from Grandmother. Jamail thought about her words throughout the following days. The more he visualized angels surrounding him, the less he felt afraid.

"I prayed a lot," Jamail said. "I asked God to give me courage. I knew that He was the only one who could help me. But then I began to realize that if God was with me, that was more than enough. I began to feel better."

One windy day in March, Jamail sensed that the day was going to be different. He felt both anticipation and a nervousness. Later, as he walked down the school hall he saw the boy from the street approaching him with a couple of his friends. Jamail knew something was going to happen.

"I began to imagine angels around me," Jamail recalled. "It almost felt like it was not me walking down the hall, but someone else."

As the thugs came closer, the bully hissed at Jamail, "You gutless piece of [trash]. I'm going to get your sister today!"

Jamail's fists struck with surprising quickness in the face of the bully. Jamail had lunged forward with the rapid succession of blows, knocking the stunned boy on his back.

Other students were quickly gathering in disbelief. Jamail stood over his Goliath, yelling, "Get up and fight me. Leave my sister alone!"

The bully slowly got up and surprisingly did not strike back. A second later, however, the boy pulled a knife and flashed it at Jamail.

The two stared at each other. Jamail did not waver and looked intently into the eyes of his antagonist. Finally, the bully put his knife up and walked away.

Jamail instantly became a school celebrity. Fortunately, however, the situation was resolved and there was no more trouble. "I have thanked God many times for helping me," said Jamail. "Angels were with me that day when I trusted God in a greater way than I ever had before."

Tapping Into God's Power

The successful adolescents we researched gained strength, support, and peace of mind by drawing from a higher power greater than themselves. The formula for their ability to draw from this spiritual reservoir was a three-step process.

First, they believed in the presence of a higher power that would operate in their personal lives. To them, this spiritual influence was more than a theory or theological issue. It was personal and was a practical influence in their day-to-day lives.

Second, they asked for guidance and help. They had ongoing spiritual conversations in the form of prayer and meditation, which helped them to experience a closer relationship with God.

Third, they trusted in God to help them. They learned to turn over their problems and concerns and then to depend upon Him to guide them and help them to deal successfully with all aspects of their lives.

One person who knew how to tap into the power of God was an athlete who was not as naturally talented as many of his contemporaries. In fact, some said he was not good enough to play college football. Many college coaches overlooked him in the recruiting process. Auburn University made him a walk-on offer, which meant he could try out for the team, but they couldn't guarantee him a scholarship. Finally, the University of Alabama gave him a full scholarship to play football.

Through hard work and perseverance, he got a chance to be Alabama's starting quarterback during the latter part of his freshman year. During most of the four years in which he was the starting quarterback at Alabama he was criticized: "He's too slow," "He can't pass," "He can't handle the ball well." Even though he played consistently well, some labeled him as an underachiever. Many called him "just an average" player.

In spite of the criticisms, he remained focused on his goals. Jay Barker kept getting better, and he became the winningest quarterback in the history of the University of Alabama. In 1994, he was a candidate for the Heisman Trophy and received the Johnny Unitas Golden Arm Award, which honors college football's best quarterback.

Time after time, he had led Alabama back from the brink of defeat against teams who were favored to win. The way he did it was impressive. He did it with poise, by inspiring the confidence of his teammates, and by projecting optimism.

Where did this poise, inspiration, and optimism come from? For Jay, these things largely came from his spiritual faith. Jay is a devout Christian, and he relied on his religious beliefs to carry him through criticism and injuries.

"He has a strong faith," said Tommy Deas, one of his teammates. "He shows it every day through all adversity. People can talk about him, call him everything . . . and he'll keep on smiling and keep on walking. That inspires me. He pulls it off week-in and week-out. He never loses his faith."[2]

A Sense of Purpose

Nothing is as powerful as a focused sense of purpose. "Fire the heart with where you want to go and what you want to be," said Norman Vincent Peale. "Get it so deeply fixed in your unconscious that you will not take no for an answer, then your entire personality will follow where your heart leads."[3]

Laverne is sixteen, and she has a dream. The dream started soon after her best friend was killed in a drive-by shooting in Los Angeles.

"I cried until I ran out of tears," Laverne recalled. "I was dangerously angry and I wanted revenge. I wanted to kill the people who had killed my friend."

When Laverne was asked what had changed her mind, she replied, "One day, my aunt, who I have always been close to, asked me if I believed in God and what Jesus taught. I replied, 'You know that I believe in God and in what Jesus taught. Why do you ask?' "

"My aunt said, 'Laverne, Jesus taught us to turn the other cheek when someone offends us and that we should return good for evil. Why do you think God wants us to live like that?'

"I could not answer her. When she knew I was not going to say anything, my aunt continued, 'We return good for evil for *our own good.* If we just take revenge and return evil for evil, we bring more pain to ourselves and to others, and we keep the evil going 'round and 'round. You can't bring your friend back. But you can do something to make the lives of other people better.' "

Laverne thought about what her aunt said for a long time. What could she do to make a difference? Finally she concluded that if life could be improved in the inner city, fewer terrible things—such as drive-by shootings—would happen.

"I volunteered at a shelter in the city," said Laverne. "I work with children, families, abused women, and young single mothers. As a result of my work, I have made a positive difference in the lives of some of those people."

But this is only the first step for Laverne. She envisions a bigger plan for her life. "My dream is to start an inner-city program that would offer child care, parent education, legal services, medical services, and spiritual counseling," she said. "The need is so great that I know it would work. I'm preparing myself to do this by majoring in family relations and child development in college."

Laverne has fired her heart with a purpose. That sense of purpose has given her life direction and has helped to heal the emotional hurt and the hate she had experienced.

Empowering Relationships

High-wellness teens in the National Adolescent Wellness Research Project are involved in relationships with others that are typically positive, encouraging, and supportive. Their relationships have an empowering quality about them. In other words, they bring out the best in people, emphasize individual worth, and allow the freedom for personal growth.

These positive relationships are in large part a benefit of the teenagers' spiritual faith. It's clear that people who have a vibrant, active faith often have friendships and family relationships that are influenced in good ways by their spiritual beliefs. The adolescents in our study represented many different religious faiths, and many of them said that they try to apply the principles of their religious faith to the relational aspects of their lives.

"Treating others as I would like to be treated is a very valuable guide for me," said Ashley, a fourteen-year-old in Michigan. "It covers just about everything that is important in getting along with people. Following this rule has helped me to make a lot of good friends because it has helped me to *be* a good friend."

Jan, a teen from Indiana, shared that responsibility is a value which has been especially important in her friendships. "Responsibility was always emphasized in my upbringing," she said. "To me, responsibility means you don't do anything to hurt anyone or cause them difficulty. You try to behave in a way that helps people. You know, if people were more responsible, so many teens wouldn't get pregnant and AIDS wouldn't be spreading. But it goes way beyond that—to the little everyday things of life. It includes not saying something that will hurt someone's feelings."

Eileen, a West Virginia teen, emphasized that showing genuine care for others had enriched her relationships more than anything else. "If you don't really, truly care about people, nothing you say will mean much," she said. "I think caring is the most important part of love. Caring enough to spend time with people and caring enough to listen to others has made a big difference in my family, for example. I feel sorry for some of my friends whose parents never seem to take the time to listen to them or do things with them."

Kenny, a seventeen-year-old Texan, had to overcome a natural bent toward impatience. He said, "I used to be very impatient with others, with situations, and with myself. I stayed mad and frustrated a lot. I also stayed stressed out!"

One day Kenny's father sat down with him and said, "Kenny, you are a smart person, but you are doing something that's not intelligent. You're impatient, and because you lack patience, you're making yourself and others miserable. Do you know that most religions emphasize the virtue of patience? There are reasons for that. Be smart and work on developing some patience."

"I was angry at my dad for a while," Kenny confessed. "I looked at patience as something you either had or didn't have. The idea of *developing* it took a while to sink in. Finally I had to admit Dad might be right."

Kenny decided to take his father's advice. "I read the book of Job," he said, "and decided if Job could endure the things he did and still be patient, then I could certainly be more patient with the more trivial things I faced. I also read some biographies of great people who were patient, such as Abraham Lincoln. Those examples were inspiring and helped me to see that being impatient hurt *me* the most of all."

Kenny discovered that a change soon began in him. "I practiced some tricks to improve my patience. For example, I allowed ten extra minutes when I traveled. Traffic jams aren't so terrible if you aren't late already. I carried books on tape to listen to as I drove to work. I didn't mind a red light because I was absorbed in my book."

Lynn is only eighteen years old, but she has already learned an important spiritual truth that many never learn in a lifetime. Her lesson came out of a tragic incident.

"When I was thirteen, I was raped by my uncle," Lynn shared. "He said if I told anyone he would fire my dad, who worked for him (he owned a large auto shop). He also said he would deny everything, and it would be my word against his. He threatened that he would make me look like a crazy person."

Lynn did not tell anyone what had happened. She needed to talk, but she did not feel that she could. She feared her uncle.

"I was so ashamed," she said. "I felt like old, dirty baggage. I hated him for what he had done to me. I went through periods of being very angry and other times of being very depressed."

Lynn's resentment grew to the point that her hatred for her uncle was the total focus of her thoughts. She could not sleep well. Her appetite had decreased so much that she was losing significant amounts of weight.

"I knew I could not go on carrying that hate," she said. "I had to get rid of it or it would completely destroy me. There was no person who could help me get rid of the hate I felt, and I knew I could not do it by myself."

Lynn prayed with all her heart. "I said, 'God, I know you can help me to forgive. Help me to let go of this hate! I want to let it go. Help me to truly forgive this man.' It was a long time before I really meant it even a little. But I kept forgiving him in my prayers.

"I reminded myself over and over of Jesus' answer to the question of how many times we should forgive someone who does wrong to us. His answer was that we should forgive not seven times but seventy times seven. I calculated that is four hundred and ninety times. That example helped me to stay with it until I began to really mean it when I prayed for help to forgive my uncle. One day, I realized to my surprise that I felt less hatred and bitterness toward him."

She took another big step which was important in releasing her from the horrible feelings she had experienced. "My uncle had entered the hospital with cancer," she said. "I decided to go see him. When I walked in the door, he looked shocked to see me. I asked how he was doing. We talked a few minutes about his illness, and he seemed uncomfortable that I was there, alone with him."

Lynn confronted him about what he had done. She told him the terrible feelings she had endured after she had been raped. She spoke frankly of the depression, anger, and hatred she had felt because of what he had done to her.

"I then told him that through God's help I had forgiven him," said Lynn. "I looked straight into his eyes and told him that the responsibility for what had happened was on his shoulders. I said to him that I was letting it go and was not going to allow the memory of what happened to hurt me anymore. I told him that I hoped God would touch his life and give him peace. As I turned and walked out the door, I heard him say, 'I'm sorry.' "

Lynn began to experience peace and contentment that she had not known since the rape had occurred. She had, through much prayer, successfully let go of the pain and hatred, and she truly forgave.

Part of Something Larger

Desire to be part of something larger than ourselves is universal. Many psychologists tell us it is one of the deepest needs human beings have. The successful adolescents in our research often mentioned this aspect of their spiritual faith as being a significant source of strength in their daily living.

"I know that I am not alone," said Forest. "There is something far greater than my abilities and intelligence. That higher being cares about me. I am part of that higher being, and I receive guidance and help for every part of my life. Knowing that I have that strength and love to draw from is very comforting."

Tricia, a native of Florida, commented, "My faith in God helps me to feel that I am part of a larger whole. It has helped me to become less self-centered. I reach out to people more because of my spiritual belief that I am connected to other people. I am more considerate of the feelings of others."

The life experiences of the successful teens indicate that the spiritual dimension enlarges the perspective of adolescents and helps to create a greater sense of connectedness. It is a force that counteracts loneliness.

A number of adolescents experience a feeling of being part of a larger whole by devoting themselves to a cause. Sixteen-year-old Paul and a group of his friends joined some adults from the Red Cross and worked to help the victims of a midwestern tornado. "We made a difference," said Paul, "and those people who lost their homes will never forget that."

Each week, Janelle and her younger sister visit the elderly in a nursing home. "Our visits mean so much to them," Janelle said. "It makes you feel good to bring a little sunshine into other people's lives. What really matters in life is loving and helping each other."

Libby, a teen from Oregon, sums it up well: "When I help people, I feel the happiest. But I have to make an effort to do it. Everything all around us urges us to make lots of money. It's refreshing to get out of that tiny, selfish shell and be connected to a greater purpose in life."

Ways to Help Your Teen Succeed

1. Be an example. Most children adopt the faith of the adults in their lives by watching how these older people live. Your teenager is no exception. If belief in God is important to you, help your children to see that belief. Acknowledge God in your everyday life. Talk with your teen about God's guidance and protection in your life—in specific instances. Please don't preach mini-sermons. Instead, let your child—by what you say and *do*—see your faith at work in your life.

2. Make prayer, meditation, and contemplation a part of your life. Some people like to wake up thirty minutes earlier to have a quiet time to read Scripture or inspirational literature, to meditate, to pray about concerns. Others find some time each week to walk in the woods or along the creek or to work in the garden and to contemplate life and nature. They find lessons for living in nature and inspiration and encouragement in the lives of others.

3. Develop a sense of purpose in your own life and communicate it to your teen. Have you figured out what you are supposed to be doing with your life? Did you have an experience that helped you gain purpose and focus? Talk about these things with your teen and be honest with him or her. If you had to struggle before you found your way, tell your story. Encourage your teen to try different fields and to speak with adults who are involved in activities that hold interest for him or her.

4. Set an example by treating others with love and kindness. Do you treat people the way you want to be treated? Think about your relationship with your spouse. Do you treat your mate with respect and kindness? Do you gossip about the people at work? Your children learn how to act in relationships from watching you and your relationships.

5. Talk to your teen about the big picture of life. Because you have lived more years than your teen, you can help to give perspective on life: There is practical value in patience, forgiveness, and kindness, for example. Helping others makes us feel good. Truth is better than dishonesty for many reasons. Crises or bad times don't last forever. All people *are* connected to each other.

Tips for Teens Who Want to Succeed

1. Make your faith truly yours. You may live in a family with a belief in God or a higher power and you may know what your parents believe. What do you believe? Study the teachings of your religious background. Consider the values and codes of behavior that are endorsed. What are the reasons for the "rules"? Do you agree with some but not others? Can you justify your position? An important job for teens is deciding what is true for them and what they will be true to.

2. Make your beliefs real and vital. If membership in a church or synagogue is important to you, join in with enthusiasm. Get to know people there; work in the nursery or benevolence programs. Is it important to treat others with compassion? If so, practice on a daily basis: Shovel the snow from an elderly neighbor's driveway or baby-sit for a single mom so she can have an afternoon for herself.

3. Identify and affirm your life purposes. What are your driving force and purposes? Get some paper and write down things that interest you. Perhaps the things on your list could become your purposes. Maybe you have had an experience or come across a situation that made you want to act for some kind of change. Speak with trusted adults about this, because they might have some ideas that you could work on.

4. Choose friends who encourage you and build you up. Friends who believe what you believe are going to help you live up to your goals and desires. How do you treat your friends—especially girl friends and boyfriends? Be sure to treat them with respect and kindness. Treat others in the way that you want to be treated.

5. Maintain a big-picture perspective. Do you know where you stand in the big picture of life? You are not alone. Being a part of an organization that helps others may help you feel connected and not so alone. Look for things in your church or community that would be interesting and fun to do. Volunteer your time and muscle to a cause: ending world hunger, helping the disabled, stopping child abuse, preserving natural resources.

How Can I . . . ?

1. A foundational part of spiritual wellness is having a philosophy of life. The questions that follow can help to clarify your philosophy of life.

What is most important in your life? From the choices below, list in order of importance. You may add to the choices, of course. On which of these do you spend your time, effort, and money? Make another list in order of investment. Do your lists coincide? Why not?

E X A M P L E

Choices	Most important	time/energy/money
work/job/career	*relationship with God*	*work/job*
family/spouse/ children	*family (especially spouse and children)*	*family* *adventure*
having fun/good times	*nice clothes*	
helping humanity/ service to others		
relationship with God		
friends/being liked		
money/real estate		
beautiful home/ nice clothes		
adventure/not being bored		
following a moral code		

2. Identify three areas of spirituality that you would like to improve. Identify three of your strengths as well. How can you grow in each?

E X A M P L E

Needs improvement
I worry too much

What I can do
Pray about problems; trust God/ family more

Area of strength
thoughtful to others

What I can do
Get supply of cards, stationery, stamps, to send cards, letters

SEVEN

Golden Chain: Roots

There is a chain that binds us together. It is forged with the strongest of steel and endures great pressure. The high wellbeing adolescents possess it, and its presence in their lives is reflected in many ways. It is the presence of a history of meaningful relationships and traditions which forms a chain binding one generation to another.

These teenagers have roots that run deep and provide strength and stability to weather the storms of life. The roots represent a history of caring, close relationships. Roots are being part of a group and feeling that one's place in the group is important and secure. Roots involve having a clear set of values and beliefs concerning what is important in life and being guided by those values and beliefs.

Every plant must have roots in order to grow and survive. Roots hold the plant in the soil and absorb minerals and water to nourish the plant. So too must people have roots in order to grow and survive.

The presence of roots is one important reason for the health and wellness of the teens in our study. Their possession of this quality is especially meaningful in view of the growing social problems in our society. For example, the increased rootlessness of our society is certainly a contributing factor to the upward spiraling suicide rate among adolescents, which has tripled during the last thirty years. When a teenager feels isolated and that no one or anything is very important, he or she is more likely to feel unimportant and that life has little meaning.

Five important dimensions emerged as the foundation for the roots of the high-wellness teens. The remainder of this chapter will be devoted to these five principles for the development of roots.

Connectedness

According to sociologists, America has become a mass society during the last fifty years. A mass society is one that has a large population; much urbanization; and a mass production of goods, values, and lifestyles. Also, a mass society is characterized by a dominance of secondary relationships.

It is important to understand why this has such a negative effect on us. Secondary relationships are impersonal and are based upon an exchange of services. For example, as long as you provide needed service for the company where you work, there is a relationship. When you no longer provide needed services, the relationship is terminated. You are fired or retired. Secondary relationships lack caring and warmth because the system is more important than the individuals within the system. The individual's uniqueness is not recognized—the individual is very replaceable.

During the same time, there has been a corresponding decrease in primary relationships, which are more personal. Primary relationships are individual-centered relationships. The individual is considered unique and irreplaceable. Primary relationships are based upon warmth, friendship, and caring. The contrasts between the two types of relationships are presented below:[1]

Secondary Relationships	Primary Relationships
Impersonal	Personal
Lacks warmth and caring	Warm and caring
Uniqueness not recognized	Uniqueness is emphasized
Individual is replaceable	Individual is irreplaceable
Emphasis is on the system	Emphasis is on the individual
Decisions based on policy applied to system	Decisions based on what is best for individual
Legalistic and litigation oriented	Nonlegalistic, based on honesty and goodwill

The growing prevalence of secondary relationships in our society has created an environment for adolescents which is both impersonal *and* uncaring. This environment has certainly extended to the schools. As schools have consolidated for economic reasons, they have become much larger and also more impersonal, contributing to feelings of isolation and alienation among many students. In our research we found that as children progress from the seventh grade to the twelfth grade, their overall level of personal wellness drops significantly. Other researchers have also noted a decline in self-esteem and in confidence in academic abilities as children move from elementary school through the high school years. This may be explained, in part, by the fact that elementary schools are smaller. Teachers can give more individual attention to children and can express more encouragement to children in elementary school. Parents are also more involved with the child's school during the elementary years. This is in sharp contrast to the junior high and high school years in which the schools are often much larger, more impersonal, and characterized by less caring and warmth. The child's uniqueness is certainly acknowledged far less. The atmosphere is more legalistic.

Psychologists tell us that when we go for long periods of time with no primary relationships in our lives, we are likely to experience physical and emotional problems. Suicide rates, violence rates, and divorce rates are highest in environments which are dominated by the qualities of secondary relationships, such as large, urban, metropolitan areas. As mentioned earlier, the growth of secondary relationships and the decline of primary relationships in our society is certainly a major factor in the tragic increase in suicide among teens in recent years.

The adolescents who have a high degree of well-being possess something that all of us need—connectedness: to their families, to their friends, to their communities, to their God and their spiritual faith. They share a strong holistic sense of connectedness to others and to the world around them.

Because they have experienced positive, primary relationships from an early age, they enjoy relationships that are warm and loving, that acknowledge their uniqueness and enhance their self-esteem. Because they form bonds with others, it is easier for them to be thoughtful and supportive of others.

It is critical that the foundation for bonding and connectedness be established in the early years of life. It begins when a baby is held, rocked, cuddled, talked to, looked at, and has basic needs consistently met such as having their dirty diapers changed, being fed when hungry, and receiving comfort when in distress. When babies experience these important acts of caring, they receive the priceless message that they are loved and that they are surrounded by people who care for them. They learn to see the world as a good, safe place. They learn to trust.

Today, a number of child development professionals and pediatricians are concerned that many young mothers are not bonding with their babies because they are not providing these basic caring behaviors. Many of these mothers never received such caring experiences from their parents so they don't know how to provide it for their own babies. The lack of bonding and connectedness is frequently transmitted from one generation to another.

Persons who do not experience bonding are affected in their relationships with others throughout life. They may have difficulty in establishing close, positive, honest relationships. They often seem to lack the ability to care about others and may be involved in multiple divorces, con games, criminal acts, or abuse. In the extreme, they seem completely lacking in conscience and may be sociopaths such as serial killers.

For example, a common characteristic of serial killers is that they have never bonded with anyone, and therefore, their atrocious acts are more easily committed because they feel no connection—or compassion—for others.

Lance is a high school senior. He is an average student and a gifted athlete. Lance is the starting running back on the football team and is used to receiving many compliments. Many of his teammates consider him arrogant and self-centered because he projects the attitude that he is the most important player on the team and shows little interest in teamwork. He has the reputation of being interested in only one thing—himself.

He has no really close friends even though his football stardom often makes him the center of attention. Many girls are attracted to him and he has experienced numerous romantic relationships. The pattern of these relationships is exploitation and dishonesty. His purpose in the relationships is sexual conquest, which he brags about as though he has won a trophy. The emotional hurt he inflicts is of no concern to him.

During the past year, one of Lance's teammates was critically injured in an automobile accident. Also, Lance's aunt, who lives nearby, has been seriously ill with Hodgkin's disease. Lance has not visited either one.

Many problems can be predicted for Lance and for those with whom he interacts in a substantial way. He has little sense of connectedness to anyone or anything.

Feeling Needed

Tracey is the oldest child of a large single-parent family. She has four younger brothers and sisters whom she has helped to care for since she was a young child.

"My mother works at two jobs for about sixty hours a week in order to put food on the table and pay the bills," said Tracey. "I have to be the person mostly responsible for taking care of my younger brothers and sisters. I help them with their homework. We talk and I do a lot of listening. I am the 'doctor' when they get a cut or scratch or don't feel good. I play games with them when I can, like Monopoly, or cards, or hide-and-seek. I take them to school activities or to places like the zoo.

"People sometimes ask me if I resent spending so much time taking care of my brothers and sisters. No! I certainly don't resent it," Tracey emphasized. "Sure, sometimes I get aggravated and tired. But I enjoy being with them. And you know, what could I do that would be more important? They depend on me and what I do makes a difference for them and for my mother."

Talk with Tracey for a few minutes and you cannot help noticing her genuine smile and her serene manner. These might surprise many because of her busy schedule and her responsibilities. But Tracey possesses a deep happiness. One of the reasons for her happiness and serenity is that she is needed and she knows that she is needed.

At the core of the dissatisfaction of many adolescents is the emptiness of not feeling needed. And because they feel that they are not needed, it is natural for them to feel that they are not important and that life has no purpose.

The high well-being adolescents clearly feel needed. The need to be needed is met in a variety of ways. For some, like Tracey, it is met through helping the family. It may be assuming responsibility for doing certain chores. It is frequently expressed through assuming leadership positions in organizations or through volunteer work in community service activities. It may be manifested through helping a friend.

Regardless of the way they come to feel needed, the bottom line is that they do feel needed. They have a place in the grand scheme of things and they know that place is important.

A Sense of Belonging

"I guess you could say that I am a lone wolf," said Taylor. "It's not by choice. I don't feel comfortable with any particular group. I have not found a place where I am accepted."

Shawnda shared, "I go my own way. I haven't found any group where I feel like I belong. It doesn't feel good to be alone, but it feels worse to be in a group where you don't fit."

Evonne said, "I don't have a place of my own anywhere. I don't even feel like I belong in my family."

Many teens share the pain of not belonging. They experience a sense of isolation and often a sense of rejection.

Gerald was angry at himself and the world. He wanted to end the anger and hurt. He pressed the gas pedal to the floor. The speedometer rose from fifty miles per hour to sixty and then to seventy as the car sped toward the concrete sides of the river bridge. There was a sickening crash and everything in Gerald's world went black.

Three days later he opened his eyes in a hospital bed. Miraculously, the car had hung on the side of the bridge after the crash and Gerald had been rescued. He would live.

But a haunting question waited to be answered. What brought this seventeen-year-old to such despair that he tried to end his life?

When Gerald was ten his father was killed in an accident at work. He and his mother had grieved and struggled through several very hard years. Gradually life had begun to be normal again. Then when Gerald was sixteen, his mother remarried. This was hard for Gerald because he was close to his mother and suddenly found that he had to share her with someone else. To make matters worse, Gerald's new stepfather brought to the marriage two teenage children of his own, neither of whom Gerald liked.

Gerald felt displaced at home. His mother was devoting most of her attention to her new husband. Gerald also thought she was spending more time with her new stepchildren than was necessary. He was overwhelmed by the change and felt neglected.

Gerald had few friends. He was not involved in school activities or community groups. He did not attend church regularly and did not belong to any youth organizations. He was lonely.

The most meaningful relationship he had was with his girl friend. In her he sought the love, the acceptance, the security, and the sense of belonging he so desperately wanted. They had gone together for fourteen months and had recently become sexually intimate. Suddenly, she decided the match was not right and broke off the relationship. She began to date someone else.

Gerald was devastated. All his hopes for love and belonging were dashed. He felt rejected and totally alone. He belonged to nothing and no one. This was the despair which sent him crashing into the bridge.

The high well-being teens experience a strong sense of belonging. What is it that makes them feel that they belong? Although this is not an easy question, these teens have given some helpful answers.

These youngsters are in social environments (whether it be family, school, church, youth groups, athletic teams, or a group of friends) where they perceive they are accepted and valued. They sense that others in their social environments are committed to them and are interested in them. Their sense of belonging is enhanced by the fact that they are involved and believe they are making needed contributions. They are also committed to the group.

For many, there may be only one or two social environments from which they derive a sense of belonging. For others, the belonging may be experienced in several social environments.

Yoli is one of many teens who has found very few social environments at school which provide her with a high sense of belonging. However, she did find one which was very meaningful because it reflected a strong personal interest.

"I tried to be involved in different groups at school—like the newspaper staff, chess club, and student council. I was a cheerleader for a year. But I just never felt very comfortable or like I had a place in any of these groups," she said. "Maybe it was because I never felt needed. It could be because they were very competitive. Everything was so conditional on performance.

"Other than from my family, I have gotten the greatest feeling of belonging from my art class," shared Yoli. "I love art and

I do it because I enjoy it. I don't worry about performance or trying to satisfy someone else's expectations. And the other people in the class feel the same way, I think. The chemistry is really good in the group. We encourage each other. We have a lot of fun, too. A good group spirit and identity has come about. We call ourselves the Art Renaissance Posse!"

Many of the high-wellness teens told us that finding the social environments from which they derived a strong sense of belonging was not easy. They had to be persistent in looking before they found the one which had the right individual fit. Much of their effort was trial and error. However, they were more often successful when they were involved with groups as a result of their personal interests and talents. Common interests among group members serve to create a sense of connection. Feeling that their ideas were accepted and their talents were appreciated helped to increase feelings of belonging to a group.

It is not necessary to be involved in *many* social environments which provide a sense of belonging. But it is important for the adolescent to have *some* social environments which provide a strong sense of belonging. The family is the most crucial of all the social environments in meeting the need for belonging. In the family, teens develop the skills and resources for successfully becoming a part of other groups. Also, adolescents who receive a strong sense of belonging from their families are much less likely to be devastated when they do not experience an immediate sense of belonging from other social environments. The family acts as a buffer from isolation.

Identity

The four larger boys were taunting and bullying the smaller boy, Jerry. They did not like him. In fact, Jerry was disliked by many at this midwestern high school. Jerry was often loud, abrasive, and immature. Consequently, he was a favorite target for pranks or jokes.

What the four boys were doing now had gone beyond a joke or a prank. They were intent on humiliating him. They hit him and pushed him to the ground repeatedly. He tried to fight back but was no match for them. He was crying. They were laughing and jeering. The incident had attracted an audience of other students, some of whom also laughed. None of them made any attempt to stop the abuse or to help Jerry.

Finally, one of the students pushed through the crowd of onlookers and came to Jerry's rescue. He told the bullies to back off. When they continued, he pushed them back. A fight then erupted between him and the four bullies. The fight was soon broken up by school officials.

What set this courageous teen apart from the onlookers who did nothing or who joined in the taunting? Why did he go against the odds to help someone who was unpopular? Not only did he risk physical harm, but he defied the accepted practice in that school's culture.

The music was getting louder and it seemed that people were arriving every minute at the large, beautiful home set on extensive, well-landscaped grounds. The parents had removed themselves completely from the party.

Word had circulated around school that this was *the* party of the year to attend. Everyone was going to be there.

As the party progressed, drug use became a major focus of the activities. A number of the students considered to be in the school's "inner circle" were bringing the drugs. Randy was offered a choice of marijuana or cocaine. He declined, indicating a soda was all he wanted. The teens who had offered Randy the drugs looked at him quizzically. They asked if he wanted some later. His reply was no. They assured him that the drugs were excellent. Randy told them that he did not do drugs. They seemed a little irritated. As they walked off, one turned and said, "You're weird, you know that?" Randy smiled and said, "That's all right. I'm okay with it."

What enabled Randy to decline the offer of drugs? Why was he able to resist the peer pressure while others were succumbing to it?

Jayne and Sean had been going together for six months. Their relationship was a serious one. They were very much in love with each other. Their relationship had progressed to the stage that Sean thought they should be having sexual intercourse. He had been pushing Jayne very hard to come to his point of view. Sean had chided Jayne for being "old-fashioned" and had questioned her love for him. He had argued that they planned to marry in time anyway.

Jayne was not ready to establish full sexual relations and had resisted. She has a foundation of strongly held Christian values that have led her to the conviction that sexual relations are best reserved for the marriage relationship. As a result, she believes it is very important to wait even though she was very much in love with Sean and very attracted to him physically.

Although this situation was emotionally draining for Jayne, she stood firm. She repeatedly told Sean that it was very important to her to save the sexual relationship for marriage. Jayne shared with Sean that her values were a vital part of her and that it was important that she be true to those values.

Sean and Jayne soon decided to break up. The break up was emotionally distressing for Jayne, but she gradually recovered. She then established a new relationship with someone with whom she is more compatible.

What gave Jayne the strength to be true to her own values? How was she able to withstand enormous pressure from someone for whom she cared deeply?

In these three cases the high-wellness adolescents—Jayne, Randy, and the teen who came to Jerry's rescue—were distinguished by a common quality which greatly influenced their actions. All three possessed a strong sense of personal identity. Such a strong sense of personal identity is a common characteristic of the high well-being adolescents. They know who they are and have a clear set of values, which they honor. Their sense of right and wrong guides their behavior. These adolescents have a healthy, positive self-esteem. They are secure enough in their self-esteem that they do not feel a great need to conform to their peer group for acceptance as so many adolescents do. They are "their own person" and enjoy a healthy independence.

A Sense of Community

"I know a lot of people in my community. I know if I needed help, there would be someone who would be there for me."

"It's a friendly neighborhood. I have many friends on the block who are part of my daily life."

"People can count on each other here. It gives me a secure feeling."

The high-wellness adolescents enjoy a strong sense of community. They experience a meaningful fellowship with a group of persons with whom they share common purposes and interests.

For many of these teens, their sense of community came from the immediate neighborhood in which they lived. For others, the sense of community came from their schools or a school organization or group in which they participated. Many experienced a sense of community from their churches or synagogues. Of course, their small circle of friends was an important source of this feeling, too.

Whatever the source, the high-wellness teens experienced community. In other words, they interacted with people who cared about them and were supportive of them. They believed there were many people in these groups who would help them if they needed it.

Sherry is an unusual eighteen-year-old in the Midwest. Her energy is impressive as she goes to the senior citizens center and volunteers for about fifteen hours each week. She also visits some of the residents of the local nursing home on a regular basis. She has enjoyed considerable success in finding well-qualified older persons to serve as tutors for children who were doing poorly in school. Most of the children's performance in school has markedly improved. A major benefit for the children is that the relationship with their senior mentor evolved into a genuine friendship. For many, their new, elder friend has become like a grandparent to them. For some of the children it is the most caring relationship they have known. The older persons serving as tutors for the children benefit also. They experience reduced loneliness and isolation. They receive companionship, purpose, and meaning to their lives.

It is apparent that a strong sense of purpose fuels the energy which Sherry has demonstrated in working with older persons and helping to create such a successful tutoring program. We asked her what had motivated her to spend her time in this way.

"What first got me interested," she said, "was my own grandfather. I was always close to him. He gradually became disabled from rheumatoid arthritis until he finally became bedridden.

"One of the most disappointing things that happened during

that time was the way people at the church we had been attending treated my grandfather. He had always been a very religious man and attending church had been important to him. But now he was not physically able to attend church and his church wouldn't come to him. He was not visited by the ministers, the elders, or really anyone from that church. They acted as though my grandfather did not exist anymore. We decided it was time to find a new church."

Sherry enthusiastically shared, "We discovered another church that genuinely cared about people. They offered a wonderful program for older persons. They provided good companionship and coordinated many needed services for the elderly.

"I appreciated so much what this church did for my grandfather," she said. "And I saw that there were so many other older persons who had as great or a greater need than my grandfather. So I decided to become involved in our new church as a volunteer to help improve the quality of life for older persons."

Sherry gradually expanded her efforts to the senior citizens center, the nursing home, and other groups in the community which shared the common goal of serving the elderly. "I feel a very special bond and closeness to these people," said Sherry, "because we are working together for a very important purpose." For Sherry, it is a purpose that has great personal meaning to her.

As illustrated by Sherry, the high-wellness adolescents' community bonds are highlighted by sharing a sense of purpose with others in their community environment. They experience a feeling of kinship by pursuing a common goal or interest. This sense of purpose which is experienced in the community context fulfills a deep psychological need. It provides a sense of being a part of something larger than they are individually. This is important because it reduces isolation. It leads to behavior which is less self-centered. It encourages reaching out to others and concern for others. It is vital to the strength and stability of our society that some members of society possess this quality. Without it, we would be nothing more than a collection of self-seeking, isolated individuals with no concern for others or for a common good. The high-wellness teens represent a nucleus of hope for the future of our society.

Ways to Help Your Teen Succeed

1. **Talk about your family history.** Show pictures from albums and tell stories. Write down or tape-record the stories. Most children want to know what kind of people their relatives were and they want to know something about what their relatives felt was important. Take time to talk about when your children were babies and look at pictures together. Talk about when they were born. Tell about the first day of school, the big snowstorm, pets, vacations.

2. **Give your teen and other children things to do at home.** Include them in family discussions. Listen to their ideas and thoughts. They can do more than take out the trash. Whenever you can, use their ideas so they feel a part of the process and that they contribute to the family in important ways.

3. **Encourage your teen to be a part of different organizations.** These might include the baseball team or a music group. This could even be a group that provides some service to the community such as Meals on Wheels or Head Start Day Care.

4. **Help your teen and other children develop a sense of identity by showing who you are and what you stand for.** Talk about what your family stands for and the standards it has. Most of this is "caught" and not taught. Be yourself and don't be afraid to let your children see you in all situations. Use

television and movies that might bring up potential situations and talk about how you would handle a situation that might be similar.

5. Help your child develop a sense of community. Have your child's best friend's family over for dinner every now and then so your child can develop a relationship with his or her friend's parents as well as the friend developing a relationship with you. Take time to meet people in your neighborhood and develop relationships with them. Organize a block party with watermelon and fireworks on the Fourth of July. Be open to your child having relationships with other adults who lead groups where your child is a member.

Tips for Teens Who Want to Succeed

1. Work on finding out what is special about your family. Maybe you have a similar personality to a relative not long past. Ask questions and ask to see pictures. Enjoy what makes your family unique. Your parents and grandparents were not always "old people"! Find out what they were like as teens or young adults.

2. Be helpful at home and other places where you are working (church or community groups). Part of being connected is reaching out to others. Don't expect everyone to make the first move in making you feel at home.

3. Look over your interests and see if there are groups that you could be a part of to explore those interests. You would not only be exploring your interests, but you would be finding people with like minds to spend time with and get to know.

4. **Before you venture out into the world tomorrow, ask yourself what you stand for and who you are.** Some people like to have "fire drills." Ask yourself, "What would I do if————: someone offers me alcohol or drugs; someone pushes for sexual intimacy; I see something I can't afford but could steal?" Decide what you will allow and what you won't allow before you get into a situation where you have to choose and the emotional pressure may be too high to think clearly. Once you have decided who you are, be yourself and don't worry about what others may think.

5. **Get to know people in your world.** Meet and begin to have relationships with people in your neighborhood. Cultivate relationships with trusted adults who lead groups where you are a member. Identify people to whom you could turn if you needed help.

How Can I . . . ?

1. **Have some "fire drills."** Think about some situations that might happen in which you will have to take a stand for your beliefs and values. Plan some "fire escapes"—some ways out of the situation.

E X A M P L E

Situation

Beer is flowing at the bonfire. No adults—you don't want to drink.

Fire Escape

Volunteer to be the designated driver.

"No, thanks. I'm on a diet—too many calories."

Leave, saying, "I've got to go. I'm sick."

2. Identify the people in your world. Start with those closest/most important to you. Sometimes it is easy to forget how many people with whom we are connected. Include people at school/work, in the neighborhood, family, and friends. Depending on your relationship with them, you might put some persons at different levels than as drawn.

EXAMPLE

1. *Family* *Best Friend*	

2. *Close, trusted friends*
   Grandparents
   Aunts, uncles, cousins	

3. *Casual friends*
   Co-workers
   Scout leader
   Minister
   Teachers
   Relatives	

4. *Neighbors*
   Teachers
   Co-workers
   Boss
   Classmates	

EIGHT
A Vision of Wellness

The odyssey which enabled us to meet four thousand high-wellness teens has given us an understanding of why these youngsters have a high degree of wellness. But the odyssey is about much more than those four thousand teens. It is also about the well-being of communities and the well-being of a society. The odyssey is about what it takes to survive and prosper. It is about how we are all connected—our communities, our families, our children and the adults whom they become. Ultimately this odyssey which you have shared with us is about hope.

The odyssey is particularly about hope because the lives of these adolescents have made it clear that it is not necessary to be free of problems in order to experience a high degree of wellness. Many of these teens have faced tremendous difficulties and obstacles, and in spite of those challenges they have prevailed.

Hope is also inspired by the fact that these high-wellness teens will be among the leaders of the future. They will exert an influence on the well-being of society in the twenty-first century. They will be role models for the future.

The Circle of Wellness

The qualities of good problem-solving skills, spiritual wellness, strong families, ability to handle stress, optimism, and roots were the foundation blocks from which adolescent wellness emerged. These qualities coincide with what other researchers examining healthy adolescents have reported. It is interesting that most of these qualities that were found to characterize high-wellness teens are lacking in adolescents with severe behavioral problems. These facts support the validity of our findings concerning adolescent well-being and emphasize the importance of these qualities, which connect and reinforce each other. Such qualities are not isolated but interact in complex ways.

Good problem-solving skills serve to reduce stress and help teens deal effectively with stressful situations. The ability to solve problems and deal effectively with stress reinforces feelings of optimism. Spiritual wellness is central to dealing effectively with stress, experiencing a sense of roots, and developing an optimistic life philosophy. Optimism, in turn, contributes to a decreased stress level and makes it possible to problem-solve more effectively. Having roots minimizes feelings of isolation and thus contributes to reduced stress and increased optimism.

Living in a strong family seems to underlie many of the other qualities. Functional families offer the greatest opportunity for adolescents to develop a sense of roots. Strong families who emphasize spiritual faith create an environment conducive to the emergence of spiritual wellness among adolescents. This powerful influence of spiritual wellness is based not only upon the religious practice or spiritual faith of the family, but also upon the caring and commitment with which family members treat each other.

The family is the institution which has the greatest potential for helping children develop the qualities necessary for achieving a high degree of wellness. So much of the foundation necessary to facilitate the lifelong process of individual self-fulfillment and personal wellness is developed within strong, healthy families.

Visualize the interaction of the characteristics as we have drawn them below:

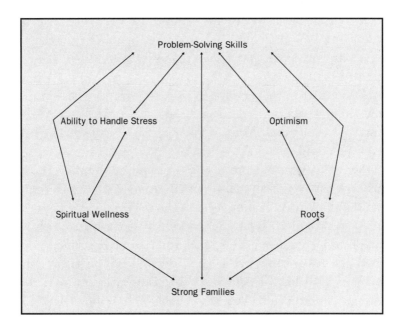

This model provides a general indication of the interactions and interconnections among the qualities contributing to a high degree of wellness. As you look at the figure, you see a circle of wellness and health. You can see how high-wellness teens energize and strengthen others who come within their circle of influence.

Can a Problem Teen Become Well?

"Listen," a concerned parent confronted us recently, "your research is interesting and makes sense. But my adolescent is a real problem. I can't seem to help him very much. Instead I bring out the worst in him and he brings out the worst in me. I wonder if there is hope for him. Can disturbed teenagers become well?"

Of course, the answer is yes! We can change. We are capable of learning new behaviors and attitudes. Some of the teens in our study had made that difficult transformation. We want to share the story of Stuart with you.

"I had a lot of anger inside," Stuart said. "I didn't realize how angry I was until it all just exploded when I was fifteen. Most of it went back to the divorce of my parents when I was seven years old.

"My father continued to live in the same community. But he was very removed from me. I wanted to spend time with him. I was supposed to visit him every other weekend, but it usually didn't work out. He'd have to work or go somewhere or the car would be in the shop. He was *always* too busy. I soon understood the real reason was he just didn't want to spend time with me. That hurt! I wanted a relationship with my father but I stopped calling him. You know, I can't think of anything he ever did to show me he loved me because he was never with me."

Stuart's relationship with his mother was better. They depended on each other. It was the two of them meeting the challenges of the world. The good relationship between Stuart and his mother began to change at about age fourteen, however. He grew more sullen and rebellious. Increasingly their interaction was focused on power struggles.

Perhaps he didn't realize that many adolescents feel uncertain and unhappy about the physical and emotional changes in their lives. At any rate, he began to blame his mother for the misery and frustration he was feeling in other parts of his life. He was facing changes he felt insecure about, and he felt no one was helping him deal with those changes. Finally, another change would trigger an eruption of dysfunctional behavior in him.

"My mother, who had not been dating anyone, met a man she liked a lot. They began to go out quite often when I was fifteen," said Stuart. "Soon they were seriously considering marriage.

"He's a nice fellow and I like him. He and I did some things together. He and my mom often asked me to go with them. But he and my mother spent hours and hours together. This scared me. Because all of those years as a child my father never had time for me. Now, suddenly my mother had less and less time for me. I can't describe to you how angry I felt about that.

"I felt that I did not belong anywhere. My dad had never wanted me around and now my mother did not have time for me. I hurt," said Stuart, "and my hurt turned to anger."

Stuart directed most of his anger toward his mother because she was the closest, most convenient person. Also, Stuart blamed his mother for his feelings of being rejected or left out. The anger reached a destructive peak one evening during a disagreement over his taking the car out to pick up his girl friend. In a rage, he shoved his mother down to the floor. Then he picked up a baseball bat, raised it in a striking stance, and came toward her.

His mother was suddenly terrified at what she saw in her

son's eyes. This was not the son she had known. She talked to him as calmly as she could and then dialed the police. He sat almost motionless until the police arrived. They warned him that he would be sent to juvenile hall if another incident happened.

A couple of weeks passed. One Saturday he and his mother had gone to town to different places and had agreed to meet at a certain time and location so that he could give her a ride home.

She was twenty minutes late in meeting him. As he waited, his feelings of rejection and abandonment rekindled. He was not important enough, he reasoned, for his mother to watch the time. By the time she arrived, his anger had reached rage proportions. As soon as she opened the car door, he sped off and left her standing in bewilderment.

Stuart returned home late that evening, went directly to his room, and began to pound holes in the wall with his fists. Fortunately, there were friends in the home. Fearing for his safety, they took action to restrain him. It took four adults to subdue him.

This event led to Stuart being admitted to a psychiatric hospital. "I received counseling that I guess I had needed for a long time," Stuart said. "It was helpful. I could see that I was blaming my mother for a lot of things that were not her fault."

Another beneficial development for Stuart is that in the following months he resolved some important issues in the relationship with his father. "My father took a renewed interest in me. Maybe it was because he felt guilty, but it was genuine and it felt good. I went to live with my dad for a while. We got reacquainted and reestablished a relationship with each other.

"One of the most healing things for me was to realize that my father did care for me and was committed to me. In fact, I decided I was lucky to have a mother and father who both cared about me. Most of the kids in the psychiatric hospital were not so fortunate."

Stuart's mom and dad began to communicate with each other in a way they had not for years. They cooperated and worked together to do what they believed was best for Stuart. They were an effective team. A real family strength of caring and commitment emerged and it was a healing influence on Stuart.

Stuart's emotions slowly began to resolve. As he began to blame his mother and father less, he developed a more positive attitude. His anger has greatly decreased and he has learned constructive, nonviolent ways of responding to frustration. "I needed to take responsibility for my problems and my life," he said. "So I focused on what I could do and what I could change. I finally understood there was no point in dwelling on things I could not change or in blaming others."

Stuart's story illustrates that adolescents can get through disturbed emotions and behavior and move toward health and wellness. A number of the teens in the National Adolescent Wellness Research Project had accomplished that transition. Many others have met great difficulty and overcome discouraging obstacles. You have met some of them in the pages of this book.

Abraham Lincoln was very successful in dealing with people and was known for his kind and gentle manner with others. One of his favorite quotations was "Judge not, that ye be not judged." As Lincoln lay dying in a bedroom of a lodging house directly across the street from Ford's Theater where John Wilkes Booth had shot him, Secretary of War Edwin Stanton commented, "There lies the most perfect ruler of men that the world has ever seen." Was it always so with Lincoln? No! As an adolescent and young adult he was very critical of others. He even engaged in the practice of writing letters or poems ridiculing people and dropping these notes on the county roads where they would certainly be found.[1]

Lincoln learned as he matured that criticism and ridicule may destroy relationships and stir up tremendous resentment. He learned this lesson when a particularly critical letter of his was published in the newspaper. The target of his ridicule, a political opponent, was so incensed by it that he searched out the anonymous letter writer's identity, and challenged him to a duel to the death. Lincoln chose swords as the weapons and practiced for three weeks. At the last moment the duelists' seconds persuaded them to let it go. We can only speculate about Lincoln's thoughts during those weeks of practice. It seems, however, that he realized the power of criticism to hurt others and that he needed to change. Lincoln did change and was transformed from a critical, ridiculing person into someone who emphasized the strengths of others and who almost never criticized anyone.

Benjamin Franklin went through a similar change. Franklin was tactless and outspoken in his youth. However, he became so positive and successful in dealing with people that he was appointed American ambassador to France. He had adopted a human relationships principle of "I will speak ill of no one . . . and speak all the good I know of everybody." The message we want to leave with you is this: Don't give up! Even though problems may seem insurmountable and behavior may appear to be irreversibly disturbed, there is hope. People can change. People do change. Circumstances change.

The Stinnetts have a bird "sanctuary" (a well-stocked feeder and a wooded yard). One of the birds we enjoy seeing is the indigo bunting, a sparrow-sized, brown bird. However, when sunlight beams upon this little bird in just the right way, tiny shafts on its feathers refract the light and it is transformed into a bird of sapphire blue so intense that it sparkles.

As with the indigo bunting, when the sunlight of love, com-

mitment, strong family relationships, a sense of roots, optimism, and hope permeate an adolescent's life, there can be a
transformation from hurt and sickness to health and wellness.
This conclusion and message is not just the dream of the au-
thors. This message is the reality of the lives of many of the
teens in our research project.

What Can We Do?

We must strengthen families. Many professionals who work with
adolescents have mistakenly emphasized that the alienation of
adolescents from their families is inevitable. As the Carnegie
report on adolescents states, this erroneous assumption over-
looks the great potential of families to promote the health and
wellness of their teenagers.

In order to promote wellness and health among adolescents
in our society, it is imperative that we create environments that
provide the sense of roots, belonging, and caring so crucial to
the emergence of wellness. Where better to do this than in the
family?

This is not idle speculation. Evidence from many research
projects tells us that low levels of family stability, warmth,
cohesion, and supportiveness are significantly related to juvenile delinquency, behavior problems, eating disorders, and un-
favorable self-concept among adolescents. Teens develop in the
most positive manner when they have a strong, supportive family life.

Our society needs, therefore, to place top priority on encouraging healthy families—families characterized by commitment,
time spent together, appreciation, the ability to deal with stress
and crises in an effective manner, spiritual wellness, and good
communication patterns. Family relationship patterns that are
strong, warm, supportive, and committed fulfill basic emo-

tional and social needs in adolescents and thus contribute to a higher level of functioning and health. Strong family relationships create an environment of stability for the family and an important sense of stability for the adolescent.

Following are recommended strategies which merit serious consideration:

1. Establish a comprehensive family life education curriculum in kindergarten through grade twelve. Human relationship skills are learned (just as math or geography). Let's teach our children to communicate effectively and kindly, to settle conflicts without violence, to nurture others, to solve problems, and to care about others.

2. Provide community-based parent education programs for pregnant teens and new parents. In Tuscaloosa, the Maude Whatley Health Center has a Parents as Teachers parenting program. A parent educator makes home visits to new parents to get to know the parents and children. In a friendly, relaxed way the parent educator teaches about the ways children grow, nutrition, immunizations, how to talk and play with babies, discipline, and other subjects of concern to the parents. The health of mother and baby are benefited through prenatal and postnatal visits and well-baby checkups.

3. Develop more family-oriented personnel policies. Flextime allows workers to vary their arrival and departure times to accommodate children's schedules. For example, Dad may work 6 A.M. to 3 P.M. in order to be home as school ends. Some companies allow two workers to share one full-time position: One works mornings and the other afternoons. Progressive companies allow longer (more than six weeks) maternity leave and also allow paternity leave.

4. Increase efforts at community and school levels to prevent teen pregnancies. Many teens are ignorant of basic information about human sexuality. They benefit by receiving information about this area of so much interest to teens, but the information needs to be complete and clear. Abstinence until after marriage should be presented as a choice that many teens might make. Certainly responsibility for decisions (sexual and otherwise) should be encouraged.

5. Implement a systematic analysis of laws, regulations, taxes, and policies concerning their impact on families. For example, persons in Alabama are considering a state lottery. Proponents of the lottery promise new revenues for the education fund. Policy analysts at the Alabama Family Alliance caution that there may be unintended consequences for the state and families, such as an increase in the number of persons with compulsive gambling problems.

6. Increase positive family role modeling and reduce violence in the media. Some of the most popular television shows—"The Cosby Show," for example, have presented models of healthy, happy families.

We must create supportive community environments. For our adolescents to prosper, we must create healthy, supportive environments in the community. Our research results tell us that adolescent wellness is closely related not only to the degree of family strength but also to the degree of community supportiveness and identity. Other researchers have found that school dropout rates are much lower for students who live in families with a high degree of social capital (positive parent-child relationships, commitment, and good communication) and who live in communities with a high degree of social capital (which is represented by supportive, helpful attitudes and behavior and a genuine concern and interest that adult members of the community have in the activities of another person's child). In contrast, school dropout rates are highest among those students whose families have a low degree of social capital and who live in a community with a low degree of social capital.[2]

Communities and families must work closely together to create caring environments with a high degree of social capital from which adolescents can draw to help them grow in wellness and health. Notice that these caring environments must be *created;* they do not "just happen." And the initiative for the creation of healthy, caring environments must come from individual families and communities. One example of this action is the work of the Rites of Passage Institute, a national organization that provides training for community leaders, teachers, and parents to enable them to work with adolescents and create a sense of community and family. Our communities must become like the northern California communities described by Wade McIntosh:

"We don't seem to get all those kinds of headaches like other areas," Wade shared. "If there's troubles in the small towns— fires, people out of work, church needed a new roof—everyone helps out. They make it work as a community."[3]

Another example of families and communities working together can be found in Lincoln, Nebraska, where a fascinating community endeavor—the Willard Community Family Strengths Program—was developed in response to a pressing community need. This particular section of Lincoln—the old Willard School District—had a disturbingly high vandalism and juvenile delinquency rate. It was the imaginative idea of Lela Watts, the director of the Willard Community Center at that time, to meet the delinquency problem with a total family approach.

A program was begun through the Willard Community Center to build the strengths and skills of the families of the youth in the neighborhood. Building self-esteem, communication skills, and expanding the scope of activities which the entire family could enjoy were among the areas of focus for the Willard Family Strengths Program.

One consequence of this program was that a spirit of teamwork emerged among the families in the community. They took the initiative and worked together to make long-overdue repairs on buildings and sidewalks. They made improvements on the community center building and also experienced an improved community pride and identity.

The most dramatic result of the Willard Family Strengths Program was that the delinquency and vandalism rates were reduced by 83 percent within a six-month period. Two years after the program was started, the delinquency and vandalism rates were reduced virtually to zero.

The Willard Family Strengths Program was not expensive or hard to implement, yet the results were astonishing. This kind of program might not be enough for a seriously crime-ridden inner-city neighborhood. However, most neighborhoods are not crime-ridden, inner-city war zones. And they could be improved by a program such as this—without a lot of red tape, cost, or difficulty.

We must create caring school environments. Experiencing a sense of involvement and belonging in school can be critical to the adolescent's level of wellness.

In our own research, we learned that among random samples of adolescents in grades seven through twelve, the highest degree of wellness is reflected by teens in the younger grade levels (grades seven and eight) while those in the higher or older grade levels (grades eleven and twelve) expressed the lowest level of wellness. Our results are consistent with the work of other researchers that shows a higher incidence of depression, drug abuse, and juvenile delinquency in late adolescence than in early adolescence.[4] Other researchers have discovered a significant decline in academic motivation and sense of academic control and mastery among students in secondary grades.[5]

One probable explanation for these findings is that as adolescents move to high school, they attend much larger schools which are more impersonal and less caring than what they experienced at the elementary or even junior high levels. This condition is due in part to the consolidation of schools, a trend which has come about because of economic reasons. We end up paying a high price in the form of social problems which emerge. Unfortunately, the adolescent typically experiences a situation in high school that is conducive to social isolation and the alienation factors which are strongly associated with a variety of adolescent problem behavior, a lower degree of self-confidence, and a diminished sense of well-being.

We can create more caring and supportive secondary school environments by employing such strategies as the following:

1. We can reverse the practice of consolidation and make schools smaller and more connected to the community. More populous communities can have two or three (or more) high schools. Students spend less time riding a bus because they live closer to the school. Students are more apt to be neighbors of their schoolmates; parents are more apt to know each other and other people's children. And, of course, it is always easier to be concerned about people we know.

2. Schools can generate more parental involvement through the use of parent volunteers and by conducting family forums. Parents can help with enrollment/registration, office chores, library, sick room, or preparation of class materials as well as ticket/concession sales at athletic events. Also, plans can be implemented for bringing students, parents, and teachers together for such activities as family-oriented assemblies, class breakfasts, and ice cream socials.

3. Schools can develop an environment of school as family. A more family-friendly school can be structured for students, parents, and employees. Entire multi-grade curriculum on the family can be developed. The entire school, as well as each class, can come to resemble a family by establishing characteristics of a strong family, such as effective communication and commitment to a group identity. One community that has successfully adopted this approach is the Family/School Community Partnership Program in Tallahassee, Florida.

4. A closer relationship to the community can be developed. For example, Big Brother and Big Sister programs can benefit adolescents by giving them an opportunity to help younger children in the community. Teens, parents, and teachers can help the community through such activities as visiting nursing homes or helping with yard chores or home repairs for the elderly. Work teams could be established in the community to help make repairs or meet other needs in the school, providing a greater sense of community-school connection. Some schools are providing facilities for day care for young children in their buildings. Teens could volunteer or work as aides in these programs. The Hanshaw Middle School located in California's Stanislaus County does an admirable job of meeting the needs of the community as well as providing educational and social opportunities for the students. The school serves as the neighborhoods' community center. The school is a resource center for the students' families. For example, parents may take computer or parenting classes or study for their high school equivalency degrees.[6]

5. Administrators, teachers, and parent volunteers can establish a visible, active presence in the daily school schedule. This practice creates a greater sense of caring in all schools and can greatly increase safety in some schools. Steve Benson's leadership as principal of Riverside Junior High School in Northport, Alabama, helped to transform a negative, impersonal environment into a caring, positive environment. One of the most important contributing influences for that transformation was that he established a very visible, active presence in the daily school schedule. Every time the bell rings for the change of classes he is in the halls visiting with students. At lunch, he is in the school cafeteria talking with students and teachers. At the end of the school day he is on the school grounds monitoring the exodus and saying good-bye to the students and greeting parents who come to pick up their children. Steve Benson is a rare principal. But the kind of results he has obtained are also rare. Few school administrators take that much time to become known to students and parents. Many say they would like to be more actively involved in their schools but can't afford to take that kind of time. Maybe we can't afford not to.

You Can't Stand a Pyramid On Its Tip

Have you ever tried to stand a pyramid on its tip? You can't do it. It will topple over every time. Yet, this is exactly the principle we often try to use in solving problems or in achieving a particular goal. We look to the federal government or the state governments to fix a problem or make life better for us. We may do that because we believe that individuals don't have the power to create a better quality of life. We may believe it takes enormous amounts of money to solve our problems and so we look to the government to give money. We wait for someone else's actions as though we are helpless while our neighborhoods, schools, and families deteriorate. Our efforts are sometimes successful in obtaining grants that help us to implement wonderful programs that improve the quality of our lives. The limitation of grants is that the money runs out after a short period of time and too often the program activity ends and life goes back to the way it was before.

We have been trying to stand a pyramid on its tip. We have looked in the wrong direction for solving problems. As a result, our efforts have been largely unsuccessful in turning the tide against crime, juvenile delinquency, violence among our youth, teen suicide, and drug abuse. No one can look at the statistics over the last thirty years and conclude that our efforts have been anything but a dismal failure.

A Revolution Is Born

We must change our thinking. Great success in increasing the health and wellness of adolescents and in solving many of our most pressing social problems is possible. That success can be achieved by each person, each individual family, and each community becoming involved and taking the initiative. It requires that each individual affirm that families are a top priority and that our children are a top priority. True success will come when individuals, families, schools, and communities form networks and work together to create environments that will generate an optimum degree of health and wellness among our children and adolescents. When the initiative to accomplish this goal is taken by families, schools, and communities, with no expectation of help or assistance from the state or federal governments or from any other source, then a revolution will have taken place.

We must turn the pyramid onto its broad base and establish a foundation of involvement of families, schools, and communities in creating environments which will enhance the wellness of our adolescents. The surge of this broad-based involvement will be powerful and will rise from the broad base of the pyramid to the tip. The movement from the foundation of the pyramid to the tip of the pyramid is the only way that true change ever takes place.

A sense of power and hope that families, schools, and communities can effectively create healthy environments will be born to replace a sense of hopelessness and ineffectiveness. We will be successful in our quest because each of us will be motivated and encouraged by the renewed awareness that "This is *our* family." "This is *our* school." "This is *our* community." "These adolescents are *our* children." "We can create the types of environments in which our adolescents can prosper and achieve a high degree of wellness. We can make a difference!"

From across our great nation, the high-wellness adolescents have shared with us their insights and experiences about what is most important in contributing to adolescent well-being. What they have shared with us transcends adolescence. They have given us wisdom concerning what is important for the survival of a society. We thank them for sharing their wisdom and for giving us the vision that many teens are doing well and that a high degree of wellness can become a reality for many more. We thank you for joining us on this odyssey. We invite you to make the vision of the high-wellness teens a reality in your family, in your school, and in your community. Your efforts will be a ripple effect extending far into the future!

More About the Adolescent Wellness Research

A sample of four thousand adolescents contributed to the research upon which this book is based. All of the adolescents were surveyed with a questionnaire. Ten percent of these adolescents were also interviewed.

The adolescents, who ranged in age from thirteen to nineteen, came from all regions of the nation. Their family backgrounds represented all economic and educational levels, many different religious persuasions, and both two-parent and single-parent families.

Several different methods were utilized for gathering the sample. A portion of the sample was obtained by running a news story about adolescents in newspapers throughout the nation including a description of the project and an invitation to participate. Another part of the sample was secured by a brief announcement describing the project and inviting participation which appeared in the *Reader's Digest.* In other studies, random samples of adolescents were obtained from school districts. The criteria for being included in yet another study were: a) being recommended by 4-H agents as being a high-wellness teen, and b) the teenagers themselves reporting a high degree of adolescent wellness. The 4-H agents were used in this one particular study as a resource for recommending high-wellness teens because of their background training in adolescence and family life and because of their extensive personal contact with adolescents and with families in the community.

The Instrument

The instrument for the National Adolescent Wellness Research Project was a questionnaire having both fixed alternatives and open-ended type questions. The questions included were based upon a review of the professional literature which suggested what might be related to adolescent wellness or health. Before the questions were submitted to adolescents they were given to a panel of judges (experts holding a doctoral or master's degree in Human Development and Family Studies). The judges were asked to evaluate each of the questions in the instrument in the following ways: a) Is the question relevant to the topic being investigated; b) Is the question clear? and c) Do other questions need to be added? After the panel of judges had responded to the instrument, a pretest was administered to a small group of adolescents and the questionnaire was refined.

The final form of the questionnaire (referred to as the Adolescent Wellness Inventory) was administered to thousands of adolescents nationally. Analysis of the research data indicated that the six qualities which the high-wellness teens had in common were: a) good problem-solving skills, b) optimism, c) spiritual wellness, d) strong families, e) ability to deal with stress effectively, and f) roots. The research results indicate that high-wellness teens express a far greater degree of each of the six qualities than do low-wellness teens. In many cases, the low-wellness teens were completely lacking in several of these qualities.

In our statistical analyses of the Adolescent Wellness Inventory, we have found each of the items reflecting the six qualities to be highly discriminating between those adolescents with a high degree of adolescent wellness and those adolescents with lower degrees of adolescent wellness. This inventory also has been found to have a high correlation with the highly validated Family Member Well-Being Index which was developed by Dr. Hamilton McCubbin of the University of Wisconsin. The Adolescent Wellness Inventory has been tested in many different studies with remarkably similar results.

Although the entire questionnaire is too long to include here, we thought you would be interested in seeing the Adolescent Wellness Inventory. Following are some of the questions we asked.

1. How would you describe yourself in terms of personal happiness?

_____very happy

_____happy

_____unhappy

_____very unhappy

2. How would you rate your physical health?

_____excellent

_____very good

_____good

_____fair

_____poor

3. I am a very lonely person at the present time.

_____strongly agree

_____agree

_____undecided

_____disagree

_____strongly disagree

4. How often have you thought about suicide?

_____very often

_____often

_____undecided

_____rarely

_____very rarely

_____never

5. How often do you use drugs?
Prescribed:
_____ very often _____ often _____ sometimes
_____ rarely _____ never

Nonprescribed (aspirin, cough syrup, laxatives):
_____ very often _____ often _____ sometimes
_____ rarely _____ never

Alcohol (beer, wine, liquor):
_____ very often _____ often _____ sometimes
_____ rarely _____ never

Other drugs (marijuana, stimulants, cocaine):
_____ very often _____ often _____ sometimes
_____ rarely _____ never

6. *How would you rate your satisfaction with most of your relation-ships?*

_____very happy

_____happy

_____undecided

_____unhappy

_____very unhappy

7. *How interested are you in learning new skills or ideas?*

_____very interested

_____interested

_____uninterested

_____very uninterested

8. *Are you concerned about the number of accidents you have experi-enced during the last year?*

_____very concerned

_____concerned

_____not concerned at all

9. *I feel that life has no meaning.*

_____strongly agree

_____agree

_____undecided

_____disagree

_____strongly disagree

10. I feel needed.

_____strongly agree

_____agree

_____undecided

_____disagree

_____strongly disagree

11. How often do you feel depressed?

_____very often

_____often

_____sometimes

_____rarely

An Action Plan

Perhaps at the present time your life or your adolescent's life does not reflect a high degree of wellness. Please don't be discouraged. Seeds of growth and wellness are at your disposal in this book. You can change the situation for your family or yourself. People *can* change when they are willing to work at it.

What do you want for your life or your adolescent's life to become in the future? Visualize what you want to see happen in your life. Decide on some goals. Plan how you can work toward them. Be patient with yourself and others. Be kind.

It may be helpful for you to develop a wellness potential action plan revolving around the six qualities characterizing our high-wellness teens. Try it! Your wellness potential action plan can be an important aid in helping your wellness potential to become reality. It can be a seed which promotes the growth of your wellness or your adolescent's wellness.

Wellness Potential Action Plan

Wellness Quality	What I Want to Happen	How I Am Going to Do It (My Strategies)	Specific Time I Will Start
Problem-Solving Skills			
Optimism			
Stress Management			
Spiritual Wellness			
Family Strengths			
Roots			

Notes

CHAPTER ONE

1. *Great Transitions: Preparing Adolescents for a New Century/Concluding Report of the Carnegie Council on Adolescent Development* (New York: Carnegie Corporation of New York, 1995).

2. Wendy Reeves, "Former Gang Member, 16, Says He's Killed Seven," *Tuscaloosa News,* September 19, 1994.

3. Wendy Reeves, "Gangs Mean Violence," *Tuscaloosa News,* September 19, 1994.

4. Rena Pederson, "Sexual Violence among Teens," *Dallas Morning News,* April 4, 1993.

CHAPTER THREE

1. *Great Transitions: Preparing Adolescents for a New Century/Concluding Report of the Carnegie Council on Adolescent Development* (New York: Carnegie Corporation of New York, 1995).

2. N. Stinnett, B. Chesser, and J. DeFrain (eds.), "In Search of Strong Families," in *Building Family Strengths: Blueprints for Action* (Lincoln: University of Nebraska Press, 1979).

3. A. E. Kahn, *Joys and Sorrows: Reflections by Pablo Casals* (New York: Simon and Schuster, 1970), p. 295.

CHAPTER FOUR

1. Norman Cousins, *Anatomy of an Illness as Perceived by the Patient* (New York: Bantam, 1981).

2. Ann Lindbergh, *Gift from the Sea* (New York: Pantheon, 1975).

3. David Elkind, *The Hurried Child* (Reading, Massachusetts: Addison-Wesley, 1981).

CHAPTER FIVE

1. David Elkind, *The Hurried Child* (Reading, Massachusetts: Addison-Wesley, 1981), pp. 64–65.

2. David Elkind, *Parenting Your Teenager* (New York: Ballentine Books, 1993).

CHAPTER SIX

1. Tara Burghart, "Boy Who Refused to Steal Dropped 14 Floors to Death," *Tuscaloosa News,* Oct. 15, 1994.

2. Tommy Deas, "Alabama Teammates Offer Support for Barker," *Tuscaloosa News,* Dec. 10, 1994.

3. Norman Vincent Peale, *The Power of Positive Thinking* (Englewood Cliffs, New Jersey: Prentice Hall, 1952).

CHAPTER SEVEN

1. L. Saxton, *The Individual, Marriage, and the Family* (Belmont, California: Wadsworth Publishing, 1986).

CHAPTER EIGHT

1. D. Carnegie, From the biography, *Lincoln the Unknown,* cited in D. Carnegie, *How to Enjoy Your Life and Your Job* (New York: Simon and Schuster, 1985).

2. J. S. Coleman, "Families and Schools," *Educational Researcher,* 16 (1987): 32–38; L. J. Bealieu, "Preparing Youth for the World of Work: A Call for Family and Community Social Capital," presentation at the Economic Development and the Food System in the U.S., Caribbean Conference, St. Croix, Feb. 14–15, 1991.

3. D. Yeadon, "California North Face," *National Geographic,* 184 (1993):48–79.

4. *Statistical Abstract of the United States 1994,* 114th edition (Washington, D.C.: United States Bureau of the Census, 1994; L. Steinberg, et al., "Authoritative Parenting and Adolescent Adjust-

ment Across Varied Ecological Niches," *Journal of Research on Adolescence,* 1 (1991):19–36.

5. J. W. Butler, et al., "An Investigation of Differences in Attitudes Between Suicidal and Nonsuicidal Student Ideators," *Adolescence,* 29 (1994):623–38.

6. *Great Transitions: Preparing Adolescents for a New Century/Concluding Report of the Carnegie Council on Adolescent Development.* (New York: Carnegie Corporation of New York, 1995).

Index